Higher Self Now!

Higher Self Now!

Accelerating Your Spiritual Evolution

William Buhlman & Susan Buhlman

Osprey Press

ISBN: 1505820626
ISBN 13: 9781505820621
Library of Congress Control Number: 2015917929
CreateSpace Independent Publishing Platform
North Charleston, South Carolina

Dedication

This book is dedicated to all explorers of consciousness. For all that are awakening to a simple truth – spirituality is experienced, not believed. To the many people and organizations that comfort the body and soul during the last hours of physical life: your gift is immeasurable. Whether you are a medical professional, social worker, grief counselor, volunteer, administrator, compassionate friend, doula, caregiver, educator, or concerned family member—yours are the helping hands that serve those in transition.

As such, a portion of the proceeds from this book will be donated to non-profit organizations that assist and comfort the dying.

Table of Contents

PART ONE

Awakening to the Infinite Journey of Soul

The reality of our afterlife is far more exciting than my humble words can express. We are all approaching a magnificent journey of consciousness beyond the body. For many of us, the time has come to expand our awareness beyond the beliefs of our youth and explore our own amazing spiritual existence. Always remember that we are powerful beings who possess the ability not only to create our current environment, but to shape our continuing existence beyond this life as well.

While living in the physical world the creative power of our thoughts is slowed by the density of matter. However, when we examine our physical surroundings we discover an amazing fact: every single object in our life was preceded by the energy of our thoughts. This is an exciting realization, because we begin to awaken to our unlimited potential and recognize that our creative abilities are expanded exponentially when we enter the subtle thought-responsive environments of the afterlife. An awe-inspiring future awaits those of us who understand how to effectively focus the infinite creative potential of our consciousness.

Throughout this book I use the term 'awakening.' I am refer-ring to the individual process of becoming aware of our immor-tal self and our continuing existence beyond all the temporary vehicles and projections of matter and form. It is the profound act of being consciously aware of our spiritual essence and our purpose for visiting this demanding training reality we call Earth. This awakening to our true self is essential to accelerate our continuing evolution now and beyond the body.

My wife, Susan, and I wrote this book with the deep desire to help inform readers about the continuing reality of our exis-tence and all that it implies. As a lifelong explorer through self-induced out-of-body experiences and meditation, I have written Part One of this book, which explores our opportunities for spiritual awakening, the multidimensional continuum of con-sciousness and the journey of soul that continues through our life, death and beyond. As a hospice volunteer and a certified end-of-life doula, Susan has written Part Two, which examines the transition we call death, suggesting a new paradigm for as-sisting our loved ones—and ourselves—in making the transi-tion experience an effective launch pad for a profound spiritual journey.

We are magnificent, creative, and eternal beings who are learning and evolving through intense physical experiences. The universal path we travel is an individual journey that begins with the courage to open our minds to question everything. The key is to awaken and become an active participant in our personal spiritual path - not just a passive believer in it.

Knowledge of our multidimensional nature and the non-physical environments we will enter helps to prepare us for our continuing journey beyond the body. Each reality we experience after death will provide us unique opportunities to learn and evolve. We have much to master in order to effectively navigate the vast thought-responsive dimensions we will experience. Our amazing adventure has just begun; let us be prepared and empowered!

William

CHAPTER 1

———— ✸ ————

Spiritual Awakening

"If you want to awaken all of humanity, then awaken yourself.
If you want to eliminate the suffering in the world, then eliminate
all that is dark and negative in yourself.
Truly, the greatest gift you have to give is that of your own self-transformation."

LAO TZU

What is Spiritual Awakening?

IS IT POSSIBLE that we have distorted the pure simplicity of spiritual awakening with our overwhelming dependence on manmade concepts? Is it possible that we have complicated spirituality by saturating our mind with a lifetime of doctrines and dogma? Maybe the truth is simple; the spiritual path is always within, patiently waiting for us to awaken to the radiance of our inner essence. Could it be that we just need to free our minds? During my out-of-body experiences I have found that spiritual awakening is not about adding additional philosophies to our life; it's about stripping away the many falsehoods that obstruct our eternal light. We become fully aware beings by ascending from belief systems and opening to the oneness of our spiritual source. This inner exploration of consciousness enables us to truly awaken to our immortal self. Spirituality is not believed or read from a book—it is experienced in our daily life.

We are all playing a temporary physical game. At birth we assimilate into a human body, gradually adapting to the cultural norms that dominate our immediate surroundings. Over the years we have become comfortable in the material environment that we call home and are conditioned to accept a host of assumptions about our existence and our place in the world. Our integration into physical society is a lifetime endeavor. We are taught to believe that we are our human bodies and that our country is our home. Day after day we compare ourselves to the people around us and inwardly declare that we are doing fine; we are fitting in and getting by. When we compare ourselves to those around us, everything seems normal. Then one day we begin to ask some soul-searching questions. What is the purpose for my life? What am I? Where did I come from before my birth? And perhaps most unsettling— what happens when I die?

Your awakening may develop due to a number of reasons: the death of a loved one, a serious illness, or a string of personal challenges that has shaken your comfortable perception of reality. Whatever the cause, you feel you have finally risen from a long sleep. You begin to pursue deeper insight to resolve those uncertainties. Instinctively you know that there is more to existence than the repetition of daily activity, the acquiring of physical objects and the clinging to an assortment of old traditions. This awakening becomes a pivotal turning point in your life. You are no longer satisfied with the status quo. You quickly discover that it can be difficult to express your driving need for answers when your family and friends have remained content to follow the established beliefs and rituals of their childhood. Many find that their loved ones don't share their burning desire for self-knowledge and soon realize that their quest is an individual path of discovery. And so begins the most important exploration of your life.

Our Journey Begins

Increasing numbers of us are no longer satisfied to blindly accept the established belief systems that dominate humanity. Instead we are questioning traditional thought and becoming bold explorers of consciousness. Spiritual awakening requires the personal courage to break from the herd mentality and open our mind to an expanded perception of reality. This means reappraising all of our comfortable assumptions. To begin it's helpful to understand that two powerful but false narratives have influenced our current ideology.

Since childhood we were taught to accept that we are our physical body. Our entire medical and educational systems state that our physical brain is the source of all consciousness. We are taught that life is a biological event that ceases at death. On the surface these conclusions appear to be logical. However, after some investigation we soon discover that there is extensive documented evidence providing a far deeper vision of our existence beyond the physical.

Another popular but flawed conclusion states that the answers to the great mysteries of life and death are not available to us, so we must depend upon manmade belief systems.

From birth we are told to have faith in the dictates of powerful institutions. The end result is that billions of people are programmed to settle for religious doctrines and the scientific theories instead of pursuing personal spiritual experiences and knowledge.

Answers Exist Beyond the Physical

Tens of thousands of NDEs and OBEs provide an expanded vision of our continuing life beyond the physical. Dr. Raymond Moody, Dr. Kenneth Ring, and others have written extensively about NDEs in many well-researched books. Decades of documentation obtained from near-death and out-of-body experiences indicate that we continue to think and function when separated from the physical body. We have gained considerable insight into the ethereal nature of our existence. States of consciousness beyond the body can be self-induced, controlled, and prolonged for extended periods of time.

A SUMMARY OF WHAT HAVE WE LEARNED FROM FORTY YEARS OF REPORTED OBEs AND NDEs

1. Consciousness continues to exist without a physical body.
2. We can think, communicate and function effectively without a biological body or brain.
3. We are not a biological being or any form-based or physical species.
4. Exiting and reentering our physical body does not require death.

5. Our natural environment (true home) is a thought-responsive nonphysical reality.
6. Our temporary biological vehicles are used to provide situations of learning and teaching in a dense environment.
7. As we prolong our out-of-body state of consciousness, our humanoid form begins to dissolve.
8. We are capable of existing in and exploring many different dimensions of energy.
9. We are highly creative nonphysical beings with the ability to mold our personal environment using focused thought.
10. Consciousness (soul) has the ability to use different temporary energy forms for its expression and experience.

The evidence is clear; we are nonphysical beings currently visiting the physical world. We are far more than bipedal human primates. This realization opens the door to an exciting and expansive vision of our existence. In fact, our current definition of life itself needs to be completely reappraised.

Religions and Spirituality

When we examine the rich history of influential religious leaders, such as Jesus, Buddha, Martin Luther, and others we discover an amazingly similarity—they were all rebels who disagreed with and opposed the dominant religious institutions of their day. They were spiritual teachers that were often persecuted and even murdered for daring to challenge the institutional power of dominant religious authorities. The German monk, Martin Luther, was excommunicated by the Catholic Church for publicly posting his

95 theses (Abuses of the Church). Gautama Buddha was born a Hindu prince but became dissatisfied with the established Hindu religion and his family's wealth. He went on to create the beautiful simplicity of The Eightfold Path and that has become the core of today's Buddhism. Jesus was publicly executed for daring to challenge the powerful Hebrew religious elite in Jerusalem, the Pharisees. Just like spiritual seekers of the past, our courage to question everything we were taught from birth is an essential step in our personal development.

It's important to recognize that Buddha was never a Buddhist and Jesus was never a Christian. They were spiritual teachers conveying a universal message. All religious texts in every culture have been modified, rewritten, and reinterpreted through the centuries. For example, Christianity started with some basic truths such as, "Love your neighbor as yourself" and "Seek first the Kingdom of God." The original teachings of many religions have become distorted by centuries of revision; by layers of institutional doctrine and dogma. The minimalism of Buddha's Eightfold Path (see Appendix) is often buried under volumes of complicated philosophies and rituals. Over the centuries, manmade religious beliefs have replaced the original emphasis on personal spiritual experiences and transformation. Today profound mystics and spiritual explorers of the past are largely replaced by religious bureaucrats and a professional priest craft.

The Spiritual Path is an Inner Journey of Consciousness

The first major step to personal spiritual empowerment is to open our minds and examine our current state of consciousness. Ask yourself some important questions: Why do you believe what you do today? What evidence supports your conclusions? What religion would you believe and support today if you were born in another country or culture? What flag would you follow and defend with your life? The response to these questions is the beginning of a life-changing quest for real enlightenment. A pivotal step is to open our mind so that we can reappraise everything we were taught to believe from birth.

The true spiritual path is invisible. It is within each of us, patiently waiting for us to awaken and travel home. Teachers throughout the ages have repeated this, but few have listened. Simply put, the spiritual path is an internal journey of consciousness. Our multidimensional nature is the inner path we travel.

Focus on Personal Awakening

So be curious. Reexamine everything you have been conditioned to believe from birth. By quieting the mind you can access the light within. Be open to your intuition and recognize that new insights, knowledge, and opportunities will support your personal awakening. Spiritual growth requires change.

Make the effort to recognize and release all the energy anchors that bind you to the limits of the physical world. Detach from the many roles and labels you hold. Let go of that dense self-identity. Recognize the ego mind for what it is: a spoiled, self-centered child who always desires its own way. Remember that we exist beyond the limits of the mind.

Learn and practice a daily method for the exploration of your consciousness. With experience you can obtain firsthand knowledge about your existence beyond matter. As you awaken to the realization that you shape your personal reality, you become energized to take complete responsibility for all of your thoughts, your deeds, and your life.

Make it a priority to become self-empowered. Realize that your entire life and death is a powerful opportunity for spiritual growth and liberation. It is a natural launch pad for transformation, if we make it so.

Becoming an Active Explorer of Consciousness

Spiritual awakening is an individual experience. There are no leaders or followers, just you and your drive for self-discovery. It may be helpful to study the practices of others, but then make a commitment to connect with your spiritual essence through personal experience rather than manmade texts. Come to a place in your mind where your quest for profound spiritual awakening replaces faith, where personal growth replaces worship. As a spiritual explorer there is no need for institutional doctrines, statues, or ornate buildings. Imagine how liberating it would be to say, "I am spiritually independent. I'm walking my individual spiritual path rather than one designed for the masses."

- Open your mind to question everything. Allow the inner connection to your immortal self to open and light your way.
- In place of blind obedience to religious text, embrace your opportunities for growth, awakening and self-knowledge through personal experience.

- Explore your purpose and path without the influence of money-driven organizations, governments, or religions.
- Rather than spending just an hour per week sitting in a building in search of spirit, you can walk your personalized spiritual path every moment of every day.
- Live an authentic life through your daily actions of love and kindness to all.
- Practice daily self-reflection, meditation, forgiveness, and personal examination.
- Experience the peace of your chosen practice in daily life.
- Have fun with it. Enjoy the entire process of personal awakening and independence from indoctrination.

We are amazing, immortal beings using temporary biological bodies for experiences on Earth. We are creative, spiritual souls who shape our reality with the focused power of our thoughts. Millions of OBEs and NDEs provide evidence of the reality of our nonphysical existence. However, it is up to each of us to eventually awaken to our enormous potential and begin our individual journey of self-discovery. A single realization becomes clear; spiritual truth is not manufactured by mankind; it is constant, unchanging, and always present within us.

CHAPTER 2

Recognizing our Physical Anchors

*"Detachment is not that you should own nothing, but
that nothing should own you."*

ALI IBN ABI TALIB

WE OFTEN FORGET that Jesus, Buddha and other great teachers
owned nothing but the clothing on their back. They were living examples of complete detachment from worldly possessions.
This concept is an established spiritual principle but it is seldom
practiced today. In our modern world filled with creature com-
forts, how do we become detached while remaining engaged in
our physical life? One approach is creating a daily practice where
you become the objective watcher of your personal life. Play a
private game of awareness where a part of you remains the dis-
passionate observer of the daily events and the dramas unfolding around you. As the observer of your life story you remain
completely objective to the swirling energies that develop. With
a clear and calm mindset you can more effectively perceive and
learn from the various life lessons presented.

Instead of instantly reacting, stop and think - what is the
lesson here? What is the purpose? I have found this to be an

enlightening exercise while opening the door to personal detachment. In many ways this daily practice supports a highly productive and self-empowered life because our priorities become more in alignment with our spiritual goals. This process allows us to recognize the incessant manipulation of the ego mind in our lives. Our expanded awareness is critically important, for we will continue to repeat our life lessons and their associated dramas in different outer forms until we resolve the unseen energy cause.

Becoming Aware of Attachments

There is an old saying: the lighter we are, the higher we travel. This especially applies to souls seeking liberation from the density of Earth. It's important to realize that nothing we do or possess exists in a vacuum. All things and energies in our life are multidimensional in nature. Our current physical existence is a dense reflection of our nonphysical reality. The ancient concept 'as above so below' is accurate. Since all energies are connected it is on us to either resolve our issues now or carry them with us into our afterlife.

Examine your state of consciousness; do the following issues influence your life today? Often, focusing the light of our awareness is sufficient to resolve or release the attachments that can hamper our growth. Self-empowerment is the art of taking complete responsibility for our entire state of consciousness.

Physical self-identity: Reflect on your self-concept; do you believe you are your body? Do you believe you are a physical human, a woman, a mother, a Christian, an American? Do you identify yourself by the physical roles you play? There is a current trend to research our national heritage, racial origin, and all of the many limbs on our physical family tree. We celebrate the festivals, clothing, food, and language of those we think were our ancestors. Pictures of long-deceased relatives hang in our homes, museums, and libraries even when there is no evidence that these individuals were in any way part of our soul group or involved in our personal journey. This is fueled by a false physical perception of who we really are. As soul we are nonphysical beings, we possess no biological structure, ethnic background or sexual identity. We are consciousness using temporary energy vehicles (bodies) for our expression in many different dimensional realities. We plan our opportunities for growth and place ourselves into various environments that will provide the lessons we need. Focusing on and identifying with our current physical race, religion, ethnic, or indigenous background is a complete diversion, for it is not our true spiritual identity.

As we awaken we realize that we alone are responsible for the anchors that bind us to the physical. How can we ever experience liberation when we remain attached to the dense limits of our biological body? Instead, begin to visualize yourself as a radiant being of clear light: pure conscious light with the unlimited creative abilities to manifest your ideal personal reality. Have the courage to shed the outer shell that holds you to the image of your physicality. You are unique, a soul who has incarnated into many bodies during many lifetimes. Your current body only serves to advance your education on Earth in this one lifetime. It is not who you really are.

Addictions, both physical and psychological: All addictions and obsessions have a nonphysical energy and consciousness component. This can manifest as anything from drugs to food, from alcohol to gambling. Any physical or emotional addiction acts as a connection holding you to the physical body and creating an obstacle to your spiritual development. What you cling to in this life can bind you to the denser realities of the astral dimension after death. Recognize that you and you alone have power over every physical decision in your life; however you must exercise this by the daily choices you make. An addiction is generally a sign of something deeper that you need to uncover and resolve. It could be childhood trauma or perhaps a continuation of a behavior pattern from a past-life experience. Once you identify the root cause, you can begin the healing process. Hypnosis, regression, or deep meditation can help. Healing begins by taking personal responsibility for your life, your state of consciousness, and developing a plan of action for positive change. No excuses.

Attachment to a physical person: People can become extraordinarily attached to each other while on Earth. Many refuse to let go of loved ones even years after death has occurred. This is caused by extreme attachment to the physical experience. Grieving the loss is normal, but unrelenting sorrow can spiritually paralyze both the living and the deceased. In some cases we are even hindering our loved one from achieving their normal progression in the afterlife by clinging to them. Energetically we are holding them close to our physical reality instead of allowing them the freedom to spiritually progress. Remind yourself that your eternal connection to this person/soul is far greater than the physical one. You came into this life with a plan for this association. If the relationship is over, whether from death or separation, then you have accomplished the point of the union. It is time for your (and their) next life lesson.

Attachment to a physical home or location: A person's house or environment can become a strong connection to the physical world. Many remain in the same home and neighborhood for their entire life even when presented with an attractive opportunity to move elsewhere. There is a comfort level and feeling of security that comes from a familiar environment. This desire is not likely to change just because a death has occurred. Hauntings are the direct result of attachment to a physical location. Ghosts are just dead people who remain emotionally connected to their past physical home. The end result is a self-imposed prison sentence for those who are psychologically attached to their past residence. In this case progress ceases for the bound soul and a state of limbo is created. This can last for centuries because linear time is not relevant.

Material objects such as a house have no lasting meaning, only the memories and activities you enjoyed during the experience. This attachment to form clearly illustrates why accurate knowledge of our multidimensional nature and our afterlife journey are critical to our continuing evolution.

Attachment to our life history: We spend decades creating our physical life story, building close relationships with our loved ones, nurturing our family, developing our talents and sharing our beliefs. Formal education goals have been met, careers have been cultivated, and we have acquired material possessions that seem important to us. These achievements symbolize the significant effort we put forth, which can make it challenging to release all that we have created. Multiplied by many lifetimes, this mindset becomes even more entrenched in the physical. The key to this is to allow the memory to remain while breaking the emotional connection. Celebrate your story, but then release it.

Past-Life Influences

Our opportunities for education extend far beyond a single lifetime in matter. Often we are influenced by a person, place, or living condition from a previous incarnation. Unknown to many, we continue to repeat our issues and lessons until they are resolved. In other words, if you died hundreds of years ago without resolving an issue with another person, you could be linked to them again. This especially applies to our personal relationships with current family members, our parents, our spouse, and our children. Our loved ones will often reflect the energy issues we continue to hold that need attention. This is why it is so important to close the loop on issues you have with others—so you can release the past and move on.

For example, during my last physical incarnation I was a German tank commander who died on the Russian front. One of my sons was also a German soldier stationed with me during the entire invasion of Russia. We both died violent deaths on a frozen battlefield near Stalingrad. In this life my son at the young age of 17 was determined to join the U.S. Marines. He went to boot camp after high school and completed two difficult combat tours in Iraq. His driving need to join the military at a young age is a classic subconscious bleed-through from his previous German soldier life experience. These kinds of unseen energy influences are common, for we are all the end result of many life experiences in different time lines. It's up to each us to become aware of the greater reality of our continuing existence or potentially repeat the same life lesson.

If you feel that you are being influenced by an unresolved past-life experience, it can be beneficial to use the services of a qualified regressionist. Once the energy connection or recurring block is identified you can take the next steps to resolve it. For many, an expert regression session provides an opportunity to resolve long standing energy issues.

A lifetime of physical challenges is but a fleeting dream when compared to our eternal journey. The recognition of our enduring life beyond the momentary façade of the physical begins to open our awareness to an empowering new perspective. We alone are responsible for our reality in every dimension we experience. When we become aware that we are using matter as a learning mechanism, it is far easier to detach from the passing dramas that surround us. This is the essential core of awakening.

When entering our future thought responsive home, our current thoughts and beliefs will determine our new destination. Our self-concept will shape our subtle energy body and our capabilities in the afterlife. At death this fixed self-identity will continue to mold and maintain our same physical-like features and self-created limits.

No matter what method of inner exploration we employ, we cannot escape our own mind. This is why confronting and purging any distorted or false self-identity, beliefs and fears is essential. In the thought-responsive environments of our home, the afterlife, we must be prepared and knowledgeable to experience our own energy projections. This begins by taking full responsibility for our thoughts and deeds now.

CHAPTER 3

Becoming Aware of our Energy Attachments

"Anger is like drinking poison and expecting the other person to die."

BUDDHA

OUR STATE OF consciousness will determine our experiences in the physical world as well as in the afterlife. It is our sacred responsibility to recognize that the path to our higher self/spiritual essence is within each of us. Eventually we must face the truth that we have created the blocks and the limits we experience and only we can clear the way.

Transformation Starts with Self-Appraisal

It's vital to recognize that all of our thoughts and feelings are forms of energy. These energies have a powerful impact, because at death our emotional and intellectual content—good, bad, or indifferent—continues with us. As such our prevailing thoughts will deeply influence the subtle thought-responsive environments we enter. When we realize that each thought and emotion has an inherent frequency to it, we can begin to recognize how this affects our personal energy field. We can look at energies such as hate, anger, and fear as heavy baggage or a dense vibration.

This is the fundamental reason why so many spiritual leaders stress the need for forgiveness while living a positive and loving life. Since our state of consciousness is the only thing we take with us at death, it is essential that our mindset be as pristine as possible. Often we operate on automatic and never reflect on our inner dialogue. To the best of your ability, step back from your daily life and become objective. Closely examine the energy content that you hold and project; what thoughts and emotions do you currently express in your life? It is estimated that we create over forty thousand thoughts a day. What kind of energy is saturating your personal energy field, body, and mind? What kind of thoughts and emotions dominate your day?

Fear: Our fears, both conscious and subconscious, create the invisible walls around us and manifest as the limits we experience in our life and in our afterlife as well. What are you afraid of: public speaking, heights, flying, being in the dark, making commitments in relationships or business, change, failure? The list is extensive. Even small fears can negatively influence your decision process and alter the entire trajectory of your life. What limits you? What is holding you back from achieving your dreams? Take a few moments and objectively examine your life from childhood. Journal all the issues you have uncovered. Acknowledging the source of fear is the first step to eliminating it. Send love to your fears and then accept them for the learning opportunity they provide you.

Anger, hate, scorn: Hate and anger only harm you; they are deadly venom you are holding in your body and mind. Understand that there is always a broader unseen energy scenario in play and there is often an essential energy balancing process at the core. Forgive all (which is not an expression of approval) in order to free yourself from a spiritually draining and self-damaging situation.

Cherokee Healing

In 2012, the Cherokee Healing Coalition sponsored a "Journey to Forgiveness and Healing" along the infamous Trail of Tears. The group walked the trail and made seven stops along the way. At each stop they created a healing circle and performed a forgiveness ceremony. A portion of soil was collected to represent their ancestors. At the end of the journey, these soil samples were placed in a cleansing river to release the ancestors of all pain and sorrow. The reason, say the elders, was so that you and future generations would not have to carry the pain.

Resentment and revenge: Make it a priority to practice forgiveness toward any person or situation and don't allow self-destructive emotions to influence you. Carrying a grudge against someone in this life can and will carry over into your afterlife as well. This dense energy keeps you attached to the physical situation or person. Create opportunities for reconciliation. This should be a priority in your life.

Jealousy: Feeling envious about someone else's life situation is misplaced energy. Not everyone is meant to win the lottery as part of their growth. It's not productive to obsess over something you don't have. Maybe you desire more wealth, beauty, or fame, but an evolved being realizes that all things are temporary in the continuing journey of soul. Instead focus on the attributes that you do possess because these create the conditions that are providing your current opportunities for growth. You are creating this reality; honor the value of it, make the most of it.

Unrelenting grief: Understand your connection to the loss, respect it, and then create a healing action or personal ceremony that assists you to resolve these feelings. (See Part Two for some examples.) Show gratitude for the time you had together rather than focusing on the premature ending that you did not anticipate. Be appreciative of the moments you shared. Recognize that since we truly never die, the separation we experience is brief. Love always continues beyond the body.

Shame, guilt, regret: You may be draining your precious energy into an event that is long gone. Whatever the cause, it is just as important to forgive yourself for any personal imperfection you may identify. Chances are that the event or relationship carried an important lesson for you or someone else. In this regard, even what you have perceived as a mistake could have been an occasion of growth. Make it a priority to appreciate it and then move on so that you don't carry those heavy energy anchors with you during your transition. There are many ways to achieve this with either a personal physical interaction or solitary ritual.

Denial, indifference, apathy: Having no feeling about something does not cut the tie that keeps you close to the physical world. It is important to acknowledge your emotions, address any open wounds, and express gratitude for all the lessons and opportunities you have been given.

THE EMOTIONAL FREQUENCY SPECTRUM

The emotions and thoughts we carry with us affect our current energy field as well as the resulting vibration we experience in the afterlife. In other words, the subtle nature of our energy body at death is influenced by our emotional makeup. It is important to note that every emotion we experience has an energy frequency. There is a world of difference between the high frequency of love and the low, heavy vibration of hate.

As an awakening soul it is up to each of us to take complete responsibility for our personal energetic composition, both external and internal. Only we have the ability to determine the emotional frequency of our energy bodies. We do this by becoming fully aware of our emotional energy makeup. This is a major component of our progress. The mastering of our energetic body is one of the fundamental initiations of an evolved being. This also explains why so many spiritual teachers stress the essential need for forgiveness and detachment.

Emotional Frequency

Our State of Consciousness and our Emotional Frequency will Influence the Reality Experienced in the Afterlife		
Emotional State at Death	**Energy Frequency**	**Potential Afterlife Environment**
Unconditional Love Joyful Enthusiastic Optimistic Serene Hopeful Merciful Sympathetic Indifferent Apathetic Fearful Prolonged Grieving Resentful Guilty Jealous Angry Vengeful Hateful Self-Loathing	*Very High* *Very Low*	**Enlightened** Realities filled with light and love promoting positive experiences. Advanced spiritual education and training leads to high mobility with the freedom to enter and explore multiple realities/heavens. **Mundane** Cloistered consensus realities and belief territories with a non-challenging and repetitive lifestyle. This is supported by rigid thinking and indoctrinated beliefs creating low spiritual mobility. **Restrictive** Confined to an unchanging physical-like perception of reality where there is no spiritual mobility. This is a world of intolerance and addictive behaviors where the inhabitants are limited to a single location or reality.

Our State of Consciousness is our Energy Frequency

The energy dynamics of the afterlife are completely different than the laws of physics in the physical world. Each thought and emotion is a specific energy frequency. Due to the subtle energetic nature inherent in nonphysical environments, focused thoughts and emotions will mold our reality in the afterlife. Because our state of consciousness determines our afterlife setting, it becomes critical for us to focus on our spiritual readiness before our transition. The energies we internalize directly influence our subtle nonphysical body and the environment we will experience after death. In fact, for over a hundred years metaphysical teachers have referred to the astral body as the emotional body.

Our thoughts can be viewed as personal energy projections that possess the creative power to shape our life. When we recognize this universal truth we can begin to take full responsibility for our individual thought projections. Any low-vibrational energy we hold, such as fear or hatred, can and will negatively influence our current life and our afterlife existence as well. Awareness of the potential energy blocks we have manifested is essential. As an awakening soul it is our task to recognize, confront, and remove the restrictive energies to which we cling. This is a central aspect of our growth because at death we carry our complete state of consciousness with us. There is no escaping this mental baggage. We create the chains that bind us to the denser energy environments of the universe and we alone are responsible for the afterlife we experience.

Mobility of Soul

Mobility of Soul/Consciousness in the Afterlife

Limited to a Single Nonphysical Reality (Heaven)	Ability to Experience Interdimensional Movement
Least Freedom of Movement	**Enhanced Freedom of Movement**
Indoctrinated physical self-identity	Non attachment to dense human form
Rigid mindset	Open minded
Follower of belief systems	Spiritual explorer
Attached to a familiar physical environment	Open to change
Many physical attachments	Detachment from material possessions
Inflexible thought patterns	Flexibility of consciousness
Negative mindset	Positive approach to challenges
Self-centered	Selfless acts
Unresolved baggage and regret	Physical life goals completed
Holding on to self-destructive thoughts	Filled with love and forgiveness

Recognize the Learning Opportunities

We are in our physical bodies to learn and grow. What are your lessons coming out of a particular experience? Every month when the managers meet at your workplace, your name does not appear on the list for promotion. You may feel frustrated, rejected, or even angry. Everything else in your life is going great—loving family, good health, and loyal friends. But this one issue is causing you great distress. How does it feel? How are you handling it? What is the underlying cause? Perhaps you are not in the ideal profession and there is something else that you've always wanted to do but were afraid to try. Is it possible that a promotion would require more hours at the office and have a negative impact on your family life? Take a look at the potential lesson, learn from it, and move on.

Maybe it's not about you at all. Everyone here is learning. When your son decides to move out of the house and backpack around Europe for a year, it is not necessarily a reflection on your parenting skills. Don't obsess over things you can't control. It is very likely that he had to learn about independence, personal responsibility, developing his own relationships, or (as upsetting as it is for you) he needed to experience some challenges.

When you find yourself in a situation you don't like, look at it as an opportunity to learn something new. Always remember that you have a choice in how you react to any situation. Learn to flow with life instead of resisting things that are different than what you had expected. Practice the art of being transparent to all the dramas that surround you.

Forgiveness

All of life's challenges are an opportunity for personal growth. As eternal beings we are playing the long game through time. Even death itself is just another page in our never-ending journey.

I think back to our first home purchase in Shreveport, Louisiana. The 1940s house had great character, with built-in book cases, original glass in the windows, and a claw-foot tub. Buying it from a friend (we'll call him 'Joe') seemed smart and safe. After all, he had remodeled this home himself and we trusted him. Within a few weeks after the purchase the decision didn't feel so smart. The electrical panel was grossly inadequate, creating a serious fire hazard, and the roof had a significant structural defect that led to major water damage. The floor with the charming creak in it turned out to have broken floor supports under the new carpet. It took many years for me to forgive Joe for putting our family in this situation until I realized that I had some responsibility in the purchase. My lesson was to be more aware in my transactions because I will have to live with the consequences. As difficult as it was, I had to thank him for giving me this insight.

Don't allow someone else's behavior become the cause for you to hold negative energy. You may not have control over what others do, but you have control of your reaction. Eventually, they will have to answer for the actions they have taken, and you will have checked off another valuable lesson.

Practice forgiveness, not just for the benefit of others but to provide a release from the resulting emotional energy blocks that you continue to hold. Let go of any unfinished business so it does not distract you from focusing on your ideal spiritual transition. Be grateful for your life and all that you have experienced and learned. Even those things that seem unpleasant are an integral element of your personal growth. Practice affirmations and other meaningful exercises on a regular basis to keep your goals at the forefront of your mind. Focus on your highest sacred intention to resolve any lingering physical and emotional blocks in your life now.

A Buddhist Prayer of Forgiveness

"If I have harmed anyone in any way either knowingly or unknowingly through my own confusions, I ask their forgiveness. If anyone has harmed me in any way either knowingly or through their own confusions, I forgive them. And if there is a situation I am not yet ready to forgive, I forgive myself for that. For all the ways that I harm myself, negate, doubt, belittle myself, judge or be unkind to myself through my own confusions, I forgive myself."

CHAPTER 4

※

The 21 Day Transformation Challenge

"No one saves us but ourselves. No one can and no one may. We ourselves must walk the path."

BUDDHA

EVERYTHING IS CONSCIOUSNESS. All physical events and relationships are consciousness expressed through matter. As we awaken we see the world for what it truly is: an amazing training ground designed for our development and evolution. Every event in our daily life, every challenge, every drama is an opportunity for personal growth and transformation. We become empowered when we recognize that we create our reality.

Self-Assessment

Examine the list below and review your current mindset. What areas of your life have you awakened? What in your life requires attention today? What fills your mind on a daily basis; what beliefs, what books and music, what thoughts and actions, what is your focus? Be objective. Are you on a daily treadmill, too busy to think about the important aspects of your existence? Observe your life and review the trajectory of your state of consciousness.

- o I have established in writing my ultimate spiritual goals for this lifetime.
- o I am beginning to recognize and eliminate the old habits, addictions, or behaviors in my life that no longer serve my goals.
- o I have a driving need to uncover the answers to the mysteries of life and the purpose for my existence.
- o I am seeing a shift in my life's priorities while releasing objects and activities that no longer support my spiritual intention.
- o I am becoming more aware of my ego mind's manipulation and control methods.
- o I am allowing my daily life to flow without resistance to change.
- o I am releasing the people and relationships in my life that no longer serve my quest.
- o I am letting go of my past history and living more in the present moment.
- o I recognize that I create my reality. Now I am taking full responsibility for my thoughts and actions.
- o I am becoming less judgmental of others.
- o I am expressing more gratitude and love in my life.
- o I see myself becoming more spiritually independent, no longer needing the approval or acceptance of others.

o I have less attachment to the physical possessions in my life.

o I practice a daily meditative exercise that resonates with me.

o I practice detachment from the energies and dramas that swirl around me.

o I am noticing increased sensitivity to subtle energies and enhanced perception abilities.

o I am experiencing an escalation in the number of dreams I remember. Some manifest as experiences involving situations of spiritual training or instruction.

o I am experiencing unconditional love in more aspects of my life.

o I have created a detailed spiritual action plan for my life and for my ideal journey at death.

o I recognize and express gratitude for the opportunities that assist in my development.

It is our great task to open to and experience spirituality in our daily lives - not just believe in it. Honor yourself for the insight that encourages you to be open to a new perspective. Then carefully examine the areas of your life that may require additional consideration.

21 DAYS OF PERSONAL REFLECTION AND TRANSFORMATION
Instead of living our life on auto pilot, we can begin our process of personal transformation by assigning thirty minutes each day for the next three weeks to closely examine and potentially enhance our state of consciousness. It is said that it takes 21

days to change a habit; the key to completely open our mind and embrace personal change. Create a journal and detail your thoughts for each day. Invest the time and do each of the exercises presented below.

Day 1 – During our busy lives, few people ever stop and ask the important questions: What am I? Why am I here? What is the purpose for my life? Where am I going at death? What is heaven? Why do I believe what I do? What evidence supports my conclusions? Write your responses to each question in detail.

Day 2 – Fully recognize that only your state of consciousness accompanies you at death. It is the only valuable and lasting asset in your entire life. All of your physical possessions are nothing but a fleeting pile of dust. What objects and events are you attached to? Currently where do you focus most of your daily attention? What can you do today to enhance your awareness? Contemplate a potential change in your priorities.

Day 3 – Once every hour throughout the day, objectively observe and record your ideas and emotions. What is the dominant tone and content of your thought stream? When you notice self-defeating or negative judgments, begin to edit them and replace them with empowering thoughts of encouragement.

Day 4 – What lessons do you continue to repeat in your life? Our personal relationships are often a lightning rod for repetition. What needs to be recognized and healed inside of you to change the dynamic and move on? Notice what issues are recurring in your life—money, health, security, trust, commitment, etc. It's important to recognize and resolve all issues or they will continue to reappear throughout our lives and into our afterlife as well.

Day 5 – What are you addicted to: coffee, cigarettes, food, sugar, drugs, money, alcohol, control? What is the unseen causal energy that this represents? Even minor addictions represent attachments to the physical body that can highly influence the vibration of our energy body now and in the afterlife. Nothing exists in a vacuum. The first step is your recognition of the repetitive issues and challenges in your life. What steps can you take today to address your concern and resolve it?

Day 6 – Examine the contents of your home. Fully recognize that every object you possess was preceded by your thoughts before it appeared in your physical environment. As you observe your personal possessions realize the creative power in each of your individual thoughts. Become fully aware how your thoughts and actions have shaped your personal reality. Meditate on your creative potential and how it impacts your life. Determine what you need to change to enhance your reality. Focus on what you want to expand in your life. Recognize that where your thoughts flow, your reality grows.

Day 7 – Our fears, both conscious and unconscious, create invisible energy walls around us that restrict our potential. What personal fears can you identify and remove today? Start with the obvious—fear of heights, commitments, public speaking etc. For example, do you hold back good ideas at your workplace because you are afraid to express yourself? Do you turn down social invitations because the idea of a relationship scares you? What fears are restricting you from reaching your full potential? Make a list; even small fears count.

Day 8 – Do you feel you were harmed by someone during your lifetime? Are there any long-standing family disputes or conflicts that you can resolve today? Can you actively reconcile with the people today? Forgive them all now. This is challenging but important, for we carry this energy with us into the afterlife. Reference the chart, *Mobility of Soul*, from Chapter three.

Day 9 – When you review your life, is there anyone you may have harmed by thought, word, or deed? Forgive yourself for any perceived damage you may have created during your life. If possible ask the individual for forgiveness. Take the time you need to release the guilt you may hold concerning a past conflict. Allow yourself to be free from the past.

Day 10 – Meditate on and journal your highest spiritual intention. Make it your primary goal and aspiration during this lifetime. You may consider this as your core affirmation. Examples are "Higher self now!" and "Spiritual essence now!" What are your primary spiritual goals for your life?

Day 11 – Make a list of all of your relationships; what lessons are present in each? What have you learned from your parents, spouse, friends, lovers, and children? What have you learned from your daily interactions? What lessons are recurring in your life? Become aware so that repetitive personal dramas can be resolved.

Day 12 – What brings you joy? How can you manifest more happiness in your life today? What decisions need to be made and what actions must be taken in order to identify and express your passion?

Day 13 – Focus on living in the present moment for one full day. Catch your thoughts every time they slide to a past or future event and immediately refocus on the present. Embrace and appreciate the miracle of the present moment in your life. Fully recognize that the present is the only moment where you can actively alter, shape and mold your life. Become aware that creation in your life occurs only in the present moment.

Day 14 – What or who challenges you at your work place? What are your potential lessons? Become completely objective as though you were an impartial observer. What are you learning from your work experiences, business colleagues, and the resulting relationships?

Day 15 – For one full day become completely transparent to all the emotional and intellectual energies that swirl around you. No likes or dislikes, just accept everything in your life for what it is. Offer no resistance or judgements in thought or deed to the opinions and convictions of others; just be.

Day 16 – Select a method of mediation or inner exploration that resonates with you and practice it for at least half an hour. Make it a daily habit.

Day 17 – Is there anything in your life that separates you from enlightenment at this moment? Meditate on this and journal your responses.

Day 18 – For one day express gratitude for all of the small joys in your daily life. Express appreciation for all you have received and for the loved ones in your life.

Day 19 – For one full day imagine that each person you encounter throughout the day is a physical expression of God, and smile. Project light and unconditional love to every person you encounter. See if you feel the difference in your state of consciousness during the day.

Day 20 – Select or create a personal mantra or affirmation and repeat it every hour throughout the entire day. Make it as meaningful as possible. Examples are, Higher Self Now! Awareness Now!

Day 21 – Create a detailed, written plan for your ideal spiritual transition at death. What is your planned preparation? What would be your final thoughts and intention? Refer to Part Two of this book for more details on creating your individual Spiritual Directive.

Our state of consciousness is constantly changing, but we often don't recognize our personal growth. At the end of your twenty-one day transformation challenge, repeat the self-assessment process. What personal shifts have you experienced? What have you released or added to your mindset and your life? Evidence of our growth can manifest in many ways. Often there are subtle adjustments that occur but remain unnoticed due to our busy lives. It can be extremely helpful to recognize our personal shifts of consciousness in our daily life in order to reinforce our awakening. Spirituality is lived, not just believed or studied.

CHAPTER 5

A Question of Enlightenment

"Enlightenment is a destructive process...
Enlightenment is the crumbling away of untruth. It's seeing through the façade of pretense. It's the complete eradication of everything we imagined to be true."

ADYASHANTI

ENLIGHTENMENT IS NEVER about adding or believing anything, for we are always connected to our eternal source. Our spiritual essence is always present, patiently waiting just beyond the many layers of our mind. By opening the doors of our perception our inner light can shine without interference. The following is a brief overview of some of the practices used to explore the potential that is present within all of us.

The Exploration of Consciousness

Meditation has become the most widely used method for the exploration of consciousness practiced today. The process of meditation is a fascinating experience that provides numerous physical and psychological benefits. It allows us an effective way to quiet the rambling ego mind that is constantly working to dominate our daily thoughts. Each day we are subjected to an unceasing stream of inner dialogue. Our intellect, along with our five senses, works tirelessly to keep us completely focused on the outer material world and our physical body. Daily dramas, challenges, and the unrelenting pursuit of our needs and desires keep us laboring through the steady churning of our mind. Meditation offers us an escape from the chains of thought. It opens the door for us to experience our eternal self—that core essence that dwells beyond our chattering mind.

During Meditation

Everyone experiences meditation differently; however, there are commonly experienced phenomena and shifts of consciousness and it is helpful to be aware of these. During our active, waking state our brain wave position is called 'beta' and operates at around 20 to 30 cycles per second. As we become still our awareness will partially defocus and detach from our five outer (biological) senses. Our breathing and heartbeat slows as we relax into a calm state. At first our body and mind may rebel and claw for attention; physical issues such as itches or pains may manifest. A stream of thoughts and needs may be begging for our attention—everything from the physical distraction of muscle aches to our mind's compulsion to review the day's activities. All of this is normal. In a sense, the ego mind wants to be the master, and stilling our thoughts through meditation is a threat to its control. When we recognize this we can allow the many physical and mental diversions to flow through us without resistance.

As we proceed in deepening our meditative state, our brain waves slow from the active waking beta state to the slower alpha state of approximately 7 to 14 cycles per second. In this light meditative state, we may begin to experience lights, images, and patterns appearing on the dark screen of our mind. Allow this imagery to flow through you without focusing your attention on it.

Moving even deeper, we enter into a theta brain wave state of about 4 to 7 cycles per second. Here the physical body may appear to be in a deeply relaxed or trance state. Our consciousness shifts further inward and away from the senses. Our physical self-concept and attachment to it dissolves and we may feel connected to a greater reality beyond substance. This can manifest as an altered state or what many call an 'expanded state of consciousness.' Energy phenomena such as inner sounds, visions, energy surges, and even a feeling of partial paralysis may be experienced.

There will be an increasing disassociation from the physical body and the physical senses. The familiar concepts of time and space seem to dissolve away. Some report that their connection to all existence is heightened while others may experience an overwhelming sense of pure love that manifests as an ocean of light or a magnificent transcendent presence. We become aware of our inner environment. When we open to our potential, the process of meditation becomes an exciting journey of exploration and self-discovery. No words can fully describe the impact of the insights and benefits we receive.

> *"I was in a deep trance state physically, although my mind was fully alert. My body felt paralyzed and rigid at the same time. I felt physical, and then suddenly I was out of body, looking down at what I had only a few seconds before thought of as myself. In that moment, I was suddenly re-birthed in the sense that I experienced*

*my eternal self. There was no doubt that I was fully
aware while fully outside of my body. I recognized myself for the first time, and that wasn't about how I looked
or what I thought or "who" I was in the world.*

*As I realized my true self, and the awareness of what was
happening registered in my consciousness, I felt tears
flowing down my face. They were tears of joy or relief
that one would feel on seeing an old long lost friend.*

*It was so familiar, yet so strange to have that feeling of
familiarity in this strange world in which I was floating.
We really are involved in some "Great Game" living as
we do in a body on this terrestrial plane. From that perspective it all becomes so different, because on some level,
unconsciously, we know all this. We know, we remember
the place where we come from; we remember living before
and dying before, and we know there is a purpose and a
meaning in it even when it seems the most hopeless, the
most absurd and the most meaningless."*

PETER G.

Methods to Explore and Enhance Consciousness

There are a wide variety of methods used around the world to
calm the mind and cultivate a spiritual awakening. Find one
that resonates with you and practice it on a regular basis. The
following is a brief overview of some popular approaches.

Silent retreats: For some, the best way to focus on awakening is to physically step away from the modern noise of the day
and create a peaceful environment. This can be achieved in a

variety of ways. You can simply clear your personal and business calendar, unplug from all of your devices, and dedicate a block of time to focus on your personal development. Some designate a space in their home or in nature that is used for the sole purpose of inner exploration. If this is not likely due to your living arrangements, self-discipline, or simply the need for a change of scenery, then schedule a retreat at a spiritual center. This is a gift to your heart by demonstrating that the connection to your higher self is a priority in your life.

Breath work: Also known as Pranayama, these breathing practices have been shown to initiate altered states, stimulate brain activity, lower stress, and reduce anxiety. There are many breath techniques available such as yogic breathing, shamanic methods, and integrative breath work. Perhaps the best known in the western world is Holotropic Breath Work, originally developed by Stanislov Grof. This has been a popular practice for several decades. It combines accelerated deep breathing with inner focus and music. With eyes closed, an individual lies on a mat and focuses on their own deep breathing to enter an altered state of consciousness. A trained helper is part of the practice to assist if needed. In addition, breath work techniques are incorporated into many yoga practices.

Yoga: Yoga is a physical, mental, and spiritual practice that dates to ancient India. Introduced to western cultures in the late 19th century, it has become increasingly popular worldwide. There are many forms of yoga from Hatha to Kundalini and all can be used to strengthen our mind-body connection. In fact the term 'yoga' refers to union or unification. Many diverse styles of yoga exist, so it is up to each of us to investigate the approach that fits comfortably with our overall objectives.

Lucid dreaming: When the sleeper becomes aware within the dream, it is referred to as a lucid dream. Today increasing numbers of people are exploring the potential of self-initiated lucid dreams as a path to self-knowledge. For many dreamers, this opens the door to new and enhanced explorations. With practice you can begin to manipulate the dream events, identify the core purpose of your life experiences, and even expand your dreams into fully conscious OBEs.

OBEs: One of the great benefits of self-initiated out-of-body experiences is they provide the opportunity to temporarily transcend the outer shell of your body, allowing you to perceive and experience beyond its dense limits. By transcending the physical body, we create an opening for a profound spiritual awakening, creating a dramatic shift of perception that can be life altering. You awaken to the multidimensional nature of yourself and the universe. Suddenly you become a knower instead of a believer; a conscious explorer of the unseen dimensions and this changes everything in your world. For detailed information on OBE self-induction, preparation and methods please refer to my first book, <u>Adventures beyond the Body</u>.

Sound technology: In the past four decades, the use of sound has become a popular method to initiate and explore altered states of consciousness. One of the most developed sound technologies enjoyed today is the use of binaural beats, often combined with various forms of music. Binaural beats are designed to synchronize the two hemispheres of the brain, thereby creating a 'frequency-following response' intended to stimulate shifts in consciousness. The use of sound technology leads to various changes in our brain waves. Today many companies and individuals are creating their own sound frequency tools and methods.

Perhaps the most well-known and researched form of binaural beat technology is Hemi-Sync®, short for hemispheric synchronization and created by the Monroe Products company in Virginia. I have personally experienced the positive results of Hemi-Sync® for many years and incorporate this technology in all of my workshops and audio programs.

Chanting/mantras: Chanting can be effective whether you prefer repetitive sounds, traditional chants, or phrases that you create as a repeated affirmation or prayer to address a specific concern. This can be focused on anything from release to protection, from manifesting to clarity, from blessing a home to focusing the mind. One purpose of chanting is to clear the mind for meditation. A popular chant for this purpose is 'OM' (pronounced 'aum'). Many feel that this sound represents the connectedness of everyone and everything—we are one.

"A practice like chanting gradually bestows on us the ability to let go of pain in our hearts. It is a way of being in the present moment."

KRISHNA MUKTANANDA

Drumming: One of the oldest methods used by early humans to initiate altered states of consciousness, drumming circles are generally informal groups that assemble with or without a facilitator. These gatherings include multiple types of percussion instruments and can eventually morph into chanting and singing. The core effect is to potentially synchronize the left and right hemispheres of the brain. It is said that this repetitive rhythm stimulates creativity and trance states, opening the door for communication with our inner guidance and higher self.

"When our hands connect with a drum that vibrates with our energy, vitality, emotion, exhilaration, hope, sensitivity, giving, sharing and unity, we become whole again."

BARRY BITTMAN, MD

Singing bowls, bells, and chimes: Throughout history, sound and music have been used to stimulate various areas of the brain. Singing bowls are made from crystal, bronze, or a combination of metal materials. The user employs a wooden wand (also known as a mallet or striker) to tap the side of the bowl and then drag the wand around the edge of the vessel, releasing a 'singing' tone. There are also chimes called 'ting-shas' that are used to focus the mind and to identify the time for meditation. There are a variety of chimes, bells, and tuning forks available. If this is something that works for you, experiment with different techniques and select the sounds that assist in your body-mind-spirit alignment.

Today there are wide variety of exploration methods available, including, fire and water ceremonies, plant medicine ceremonies and many forms of self-hypnosis just to name a few.

The exploration of consciousness is an individual inner journey. The true nature of enlightenment is about clearing away the mountain of programming that has buried the radiance of our inner spiritual essence. Meditative practices are designed to assist in this pursuit. There are many ways to experience awakening and a conscious connection with our higher self. Knowing that there are a variety of approaches will help you to select the one that is right for you. Some prefer a group setting, while others a solo activity, or a combination of both. Regardless of the method you use to support your path, be sure to practice on a daily basis. Journaling your experiences is important for it will help you to track your progress and sends a powerful message to your conscious and subconscious mind that your awakening is the top priority in your life.

CHAPTER 6

The Higher Self

"Spirit is the essence of consciousness, the energy of the universe that creates all things. Each one of us is a part of that spirit—a divine entity. So the spirit is the higher self, the eternal being that lives within us."

SHAKTI GAWAIN

FOR MANY OF us, the ultimate sacred goal is to reunite with our spiritual essence or what many today call the higher self. Over the centuries this unification experience has been revered for its ability to impart enlightenment and liberation. Writers and teachers have attempted to describe the existence of the higher self. The challenge is apparent: how can you describe something that exists beyond all three-dimensional form?

For the purpose of clarity we can describe the higher self as the essence of consciousness existing beyond the mind and the ego personalities of man; our center point that endures beyond all density, duality, beliefs, and separation. It is our essential core, that which has guided us through all of our lives, supporting our present education on Earth, and preparing us for our infinite journey. It is the very heart of our being that knows our strengths, limitations, and aspirations. It is the part of us that recognizes the unseen purpose for all of our experiences.

Our higher self extends beyond the human concepts of time, density, gender, and race. In order to function in different dense dimensions, we possess the ability to use multiple energy bodies as instruments for exploration and expression. Our spiritual essence holds the knowledge of all our collective experiences in this lifetime and all life experiences in every dimension.

A connection with our higher self can be established through meditation, daily rituals, repeating mantras, reciting affirmations, or simply having a focused, sacred time. In addition, OBEs, NDEs, and lucid dreams can open the door to this deep connection. The specifics of the method may be unique to you, but the sensation of alignment to your higher self will have commonalities that are shared across all cultural, ancestral, and religious backgrounds.

In over forty years of out-of-body travel I have had many mind-bending experiences and perceptions that are difficult to describe. How do you describe realities existing without three dimensional forms? How do you describe worlds created instantly by focused thought? Back in 1972 I had my first self-initiated OBE after three weeks of dedicated daily practice. It was a life changing event but just the beginning of my explorations of consciousness. After years of etheric and astral dimension travel this was one of my most meaningful experiences after a normal OBE self-induction.

"With a sensation of extreme inner motion, I'm thrust through layers upon layers of energy and color. It feels as if my mind is being stretched throughout the entire universe. The intense speed

is impossible to describe and just as suddenly all motion ceases. My entire being bathes in the clear light of pure presence and I feel a sense of freedom I've never dreamed possible. Complete peace and harmony saturates my being. I float in an ethereal ocean of glorious living light and I am connected to all life. No three dimensional form just an endless loving sea of pure white conscious light.

Waves of bliss and levels of love and joy saturate my awareness and I comprehend a staggering truth - I am all, connected to all, there is no separation. I am consciously connected to all that is, yet I somehow remain an individual. I feel connected to the entire expanse of the vast universe and its wisdom. Words are useless. I surrender in this experience and am saturated by an ocean of unconditional love. Upon returning to my body I am forever changed."

With patience and focused intention, an OBE can result in a profound spiritual experience. Connecting with our higher self allows us to experience a transformational shift of consciousness, enhancing our perception beyond the physical body and the ego mind. It accelerates our growth by opening us to our true self —a life-changing experience.

"At first I was dreaming about being in a store browsing around …and I began to feel myself lift off of the floor and I knew I was moving into an out-of-body experience. I thought, "I'm having an obe!" Should I just take off and fly away? I decided to go for it, so I crossed my arms over my chest and lifted off. I was soon flying/ floating over the shop still saying, "I'm out of my body.

*Where should I go?" I decided against going to see my
husband who was in another room because I didn't
want to freak him out. So I ask to go to my Higher
Self. I could feel my body become less important. It was
melting away from my center. I heard a voice telling me
"You are love. You are part of the divine." By this time
my body had pretty much dissolved away as I floated in
the most tranquil, beautiful field of nothingness. When
I came back to my body I felt at such peace – nothing
has ever felt that way again."*

MARGARET M.

Connecting with our Higher Self

As we move through the human experience, the ideal method
to experience our higher self is by way of our inner exploration
practices. For many people the concept of connecting with our
higher self is an ethereal idea. How can we connect with something existing beyond matter, mind, or duality? One approach
is to visualize an idealized image or representation that you can
identify; for example, a sphere of radiant white light, a magnificent glowing yellow sun, or any image that you may feel represents your highest aspiration in this lifetime can be effective.

CREATING A POWERFUL SPIRITUAL SYMBOL OR IMAGE

1. Sit in a comfortable position and close your eyes while
   focusing on your breath. Just completely relax and allow
   all thoughts of today to dissolve away.

2. Sincerely request that your heart provide you with a clear visual symbol or image of your higher self. Be open to all impressions without judgement.
3. In your mind's eye imagine that your higher self is in the distance and moving toward you. You may sense this in any manner that is meaningful to you. Now you are standing in front of your powerful spiritual symbol. You can feel the radiant light and energy pouring from the symbol of your higher self. Take all the time you need to visualize, open to and be with your symbol.
4. Clearly imagine and feel that you are merging with your spiritual image. You can see and feel your symbol clearly. Surrender to it; become one with it, for nothing blocks or restricts your connection. Acknowledge that there is no separation between your conscious mind and your higher self.
5. Allow your thoughts to drift away and become one with your intention to experience your higher self. Meditate on melding your awareness with your personal image. Be open to all inner shifts. Let go and flow.

During the past twenty years of my international OBE survey, thousands of people have shared their profound experiences beyond the body. This is another experience that was reported during an OBE:

> *"When my OBE experience occurred I felt myself being pulled on one side. Within moments my light increased within me exponentially and before I knew it my image of myself no longer existed and then I was off. I was moving so fast that the only speed I know of is the speed*

of light. After an instant I arrived before a blazing Sun,
it was close but I felt no sense of temperature from it.
I could see or sense light around me and an amazing
peace throughout my whole being. I was in front of the
sun for a long period of time knowing that what was
in front of me was my one true source, it wasn't even
a second thought and still isn't. I was before God, the
essence of my being. I'll never forget it, and I do believe
I am forever changed by this incredible experience. I
feel blessed knowing that I have this kind of capability
within me and have since a young age. I no longer feel
like an outsider, and now I have come to understand
the gift I carry and that others do too, that I am not
crazy, I am just awakened."

KEN C.

Your higher self will assist the intellectual part of your mind
to identify your mission or goal for this physical incarnation.
Those individuals who have blocked the inner relationship to
their higher self will often feel empty, bored, uneasy, or even
have vague feelings of remorse. If you have discovered your mission, then your higher self will confirm that you are successfully moving along the right path or, if needed, let you know that
you have wandered from it. As you nurture this internal bond,
you will feel an increasing sense of love and truth; ultimately
creating a union with your divine being. It is up to us to open to
and recognize these opportunities as they unfold in our lives.

Connecting to your higher self is important because it provides a powerful way to awaken to your life's purpose, and accomplish your mission while here in this physical body. It provides you with expanded self-awareness and a constant knowing that will transcend the mind. When connecting to your higher self during physical death, you can easily move to the highest level that is appropriate for your next phase of spiritual evolution.

CHAPTER 7

The Journey Home

"We are all visitors to this time, this place. We are just passing through. Our purpose here is to observe, to learn, to grow, to love . . . and then we return home."

AUSTRALIAN ABORIGINAL PROVERB

Earth Training

WE ARE LIVING in the most effective training environment ever conceived, the evolution of consciousness through multiple form-based realities. Earth provides an intense, educational location created to train developing consciousness in order to acquire the qualities required to enter and coexist within the higher vibrational dimensions. Our instruction is made available through personal life challenges, conflicts, drama, interactions, and relationships. We experience the recurring cause and effect of our own thoughts and actions until we awaken to the realization that we are the creators of our own lessons. We are responsible. And since we are immortal the length of time our education may take is completely irrelevant.

We are far more fascinating beings than anyone can begin to imagine. We are pure consciousness using a human body to gain experience and knowledge. We do not breathe air or possess eyes or ears. Our existence is not dependent on dense human forms or physical senses. And most importantly, there is no such thing as death, only the shedding of the outer chrysalis followed by our amazing journey beyond the dense façade of matter.

What a brilliant creation we are experiencing. Since the beginning, not a single soul has ever died. If the earth were destroyed today no one would die; instead we would automatically transfer our consciousness to our higher vibrational, less dense, energy body and continue our great spiritual quest. The earth we love is but one of millions of temporary environments designed for the training and education of soul.

Just for a moment imagine a pristine world without the need for physical life forms, time, and space. Imagine a perfect reality beyond the limiting concepts of matter and linear time. As we learn to explore beyond our body, each dimension we experience becomes increasingly thought-responsive and less dense until we enter realities beyond three-dimensional concepts.

Our True Home

Few stop to consider the composition of the magnificent environments that are our true home. We call it 'heaven,' but what is this unseen world we so universally love and desire to enter? Heaven is a series of nonphysical dimensions— countless realities that possess no physical mass or molecular structure. As we progress toward our inner spiritual source, each dimension we enter is progressively less dense and increasingly more thought-responsive.

The physics of the afterlife exist and function by a completely different set of energy laws. The energy of thought is the prevailing creative force that sustains us. We will not possess physical senses or organs such eyes, ears, or lungs; there is no air in the afterlife. Our sensory perceptions - vision, hearing, and touch - will be molded by our subconscious and conscious mind; our established self-conception will determine our external form.

One observation stands out consistently: our state of consciousness defines both our capabilities and our limits in the afterlife. For example, if you believe that you are an Asian, human male, you will continue to be so after death. We possess unlimited creative abilities; yet after death the majority of humanity will continue to cling to their last physical self-image and their corresponding earth-like perception of reality. At death humans are drawn to relatively dense vibrational realities existing close to the physical world because their loved ones are present and this kind of environment is comfortable and familiar to them.

The Arrival Experience

Most people will experience a joyful greeting from previously deceased loved ones, relatives, friends, and others who are part of their soul group. These friendly faces welcome you to their collective. Residents will appear younger, healthier, and more energetic. Our state of consciousness is transferred intact, so all of our positive and negative attributes remain. In addition, all of our values, talents, limits, and anxieties will carry over to some extent. If death is due to a sudden or tragic event, many will experience a transitional healing and recuperation area for recovery before entering any of the more residential environments. During cases of extreme and sudden violent death, some are likely to be confused or experience amnesia, so there are healers present to assist as they adjust to their new life.

Understanding the Nonphysical Realities

There are three major kinds of nonphysical environments you may encounter after your death and also during OBEs, NDEs and explorations of consciousness.

Consensus realities – After death most humans enter environments that have been created and maintained by group collective thought. Each reality is a direct manifestation of the thoughts and actions of the local population. It's common for these surroundings to be modeled upon the familiar environments from their previous physical life. For example; if in your most recent earth experience you and your family members were comfortable in a country farm house, then chances are you will meet your deceased loved ones in an area that is reflective of this physical-like reality. Depending upon the soul group you have rejoined, this could be a picturesque mountain retreat or a bustling inner city, but all are generated by group collective thought. The number and diversity of consensus realities extend beyond human imagination. At their death many souls assume that these pleasant environments are the ultimate heaven or biblical paradise. It is up to each of us to decide if the first afterlife realities we experience at death are heaven or the ultimate gilded cage. Since consensus realities are sustained by collective thought they cannot be immediately changed or altered by individual thought projections. Group consensus realities created by the shared beliefs of the inhabitants are also referred to as belief territories.

Non Consensus Realities – Nonphysical realities that are form-based but currently not energetically maintained or supported by individual or group thought. When entering these realities our focused thoughts and affirmations can potentially influence and alter these environments. Many of these existing physical-like realities have been abandoned by the local inhabitants. For example, many of the ancient temples and cities built during Earth history still exist but are no longer inhabited or supported by the thoughts of active nonphysical inhabitants. All three-dimensional objects are manifested constructs created and maintained by collective thought. Abandoned nonphysical thought forms (buildings and other structures) can potentially be manipulated by individual focused thought.

Voids – Nonphysical realities that are completely formless because collective thoughts have not shaped the energy environment. Voids are perceived as an empty space with no three dimensional form or objects – no up or down. Non form-based environments exist in every nonphysical dimension and can be very responsive to focused thought. Entering a void can be confusing when no solid reference points are present. Remain calm and focus on your primary intention. Refer to Chapter 10 for details on navigating nonphysical realities.

Understanding the core nature of the environments you will experience is essential in order to navigate within nonphysical realities and the afterlife. As we awaken to the totality of our multidimensional self, we evolve beyond the limits of the collective environments of the astral and physical dimensions and open to our unlimited potential to create our ideal reality in all dimensions.

The Myth of Eternal Hell

There is no biblical eternal hell. However, self-destructive projections of energy such as extreme anger, hate or self-loathing as we die can potentially influence and shape our afterlife experience. Since the afterlife is thought-responsive, our last dominant emotions and thoughts at the time of transition can mold the subtle energy environments we experience after death. It's important that we take full responsibility for our thought projections; no external belief system can absolve you of your own thought creations. For example, if you are agonizing over a cruel deed you committed on Earth, even if a religious leader forgave you, it will mean nothing unless you have forgiven yourself. The words of another cannot protect you from your own self judgment. Only you have the power to release the self-destructive thoughts you hold and shift into a more positive state of consciousness.

In Buddhist philosophy, the images of the wrathful deities are representative of the projections of the mind that create unpleasant experiences and environments in the afterlife. Our fear-based energies can and will manifest as negative thought-forms and manifestations. This rapid thought creation process is well documented, for it occurs during OBEs and NDEs. This is why taking full responsibility for our thoughts and beliefs is essential. I provide extensive details of this process in two of my previous books, <u>The Secret of the Soul</u>, and <u>Adventures in the Afterlife</u>.

The Physical and Astral Dimensions as a Filter for Consciousness

During the past forty years of my out-of-body explorations, I have made a startling observation: a large percentage of individuals after death remain cloistered within nonphysical realities (heavens) that exist close in vibration to the physical world. Countless billions of realities exist and each heaven is inhabited by a community of like-minded souls who have collectively manifested a very pleasant, even beautiful, physical-like environment. However, most of the inhabitants remain limited to a single dimensional reality, just like the humans on Earth. They cannot move through the established energy perimeters or barriers; they cannot fly, walk through walls or enter other dimensional environments. Many remain unaware of the vast multidimensional nature and expanse of the nonphysical universe. Due to this lack of spiritual self-knowledge, most humans continue to cling to the limits of their physical self-concept and capabilities upon entering the afterlife. Ask yourself an important question; what is heaven to you? What is your current self-conception? How can you spiritually evolve beyond your own physically indoctrinated mindset and self-created limits?

Through our intense life experiences we are educated and prepared for the instant thought responsive realities of the higher dimensions. The diverse training environments of the physical and astral dimensions function as an effective training ground and filter for the pristine higher dimensional heavens. Only the tested and evolved, who have mastered their creative thought projections are spiritually developed and evolved so they can enter and energetically coexist within the ultimate heavens. Examples of this essential spiritual training process are provided in <u>Adventures in the Afterlife</u>.

The Basic Energy Principles of Nonphysical Reality

1. All form-based realities are crystalized thought projections.
2. Our perceived reality in every dimension is relative to the energy density/frequency of the observer.
3. Focused thoughts are highly creative energy projections; they shape and mold our reality.
4. The more focused the thought projection the faster the creative effect upon surrounding energies.
5. Collective thought increases the creative effectiveness and duration of any form-based nonphysical object or reality.
6. All nonphysical realities (heavens) are created and maintained by group collective thoughts.
7. There is no molecular decay; nonphysical realities remain stable indefinitely as long as the supporting thoughts are maintained. Every imaginable environment, structure, philosophy or belief system will continue to exist as long as the inhabitants continue to support it with their thoughts.

8. Our evolution is centered on our ability to master our thought projections within every dimensional reality of the multiverse.

9. We remain cloistered within the dense epidermis layers (physical and astral dimensions) of the vast multidimensional universe until we master our thought energy projections.

Just imagine the complete havoc and destruction one primitive, undisciplined mind would create within an immaculate, instant thought responsive heaven! Who would you want standing by your side in an instant thought responsive reality? The physical and astral dimensions provide the essential training required for souls to eventually enter the higher dimensional realities (heavens).

With accurate knowledge and a spiritual action plan, we can achieve liberation from the many consensus realities that dominate the astral dimension. Our ability to obtain self-knowledge through our personal explorations of consciousness is essential to the natural trajectory and evolution of soul.

At death it is imperative to remain focused on your highest intention or goal and maintain a sense of detachment from the material world. Always remember; we possess the ability to overcome all the physical attachments that so often lure humans to the familiar afterlife realities of the astral dimension. Be bold and never settle for the mundane reflections of Earth.

It's up to us to break free of the walls of indoctrination and become an active explorer of consciousness. A pivotal shift occurs when we realize that we shape not only our current circumstance but our afterlife reality as well. We are not victims at death, we are a divine powerhouse, ready to explore, discover, and experience our spiritual self.

CHAPTER 8

Achieving Escape Velocity

"Energy, like you, has no beginning and no end. It can never be destroyed. It is only ever shifting states."

PANACHE DESAI

OVER THREE DECADES ago the concept of escape velocity was presented by the author Robert Monroe. He refers to an energy system where humans (consciousness) become trapped in a repetitive Earth-life cycle as they collect "energy". He states that each of us will eventually awaken to the absolute need to achieve escape velocity in order to break free the dense gravity field of matter and form.

It becomes clear that the Buddhist concept of liberation from the wheel of rebirth, the Monroe concept of escape velocity from the Earth life system and my descriptions of humans cloistered within the consensus realities of the physical and astral dimensions are all precisely the same unfolding dynamic - the evolution of consciousness through multiple form-based realities. This process is the multidimensional training ground of soul.

Navigating the Initial Afterlife Reality

During the first moments of death most people are met by their dead loved ones that inhabit nonphysical environments located within the astral dimension. Few ever stop to question this wonderful reunion process and most assume this is the only option available to them. However when we explore deeper we awaken to a startling truth; during this joyful unification with loved ones we have unknowingly accepted and merged our state of consciousness with the vibrational energies and consensus limits of their loved one's collective reality. Your new heavenly home is actually a physical-like reflection of Earth located within the astral dimension – these familiar dense environments exist far from your ultimate spiritual home. With your assimilation into this pleasant physical-like "heaven" you have just secured your place in a relatively dense reality within the astral dimension and have ensured your eventual reincarnation. In Adventures in the Afterlife I describe the afterlife journey and the various spiritual training opportunities in detail.

Both our physical life and our afterlife are created by the choices and actions we make. Through our expanded self-awareness and a spiritual action plan we can accelerate our evolution beyond the physical and the astral realities. We are empowered beings of pure light with the ability to enjoy liberation from the many realities of the physical and astral dimensions. By navigating the full spectrum of our inner self we can experience the higher vibrational heavens of our true spiritual home. By enhancing our current awareness we can experience escape velocity from the consensus realities and belief territories that dominate the astral dimension. As empowered spiritual beings we are never victims of fate, instead, we possess the free will to determine our trajectory of consciousness at death.

The Continuing Journey of Soul

Every birth and every death is the entry and exit of consciousness as it moves throughout this magnificent energy creation. Each dimension serves a specific purpose, providing us with unique training opportunities. It is a fool-proof system for the evolution of consciousness. Since we are immortal, the time and number of training experiences required to complete our education is irrelevant. Graduation is assured for all.

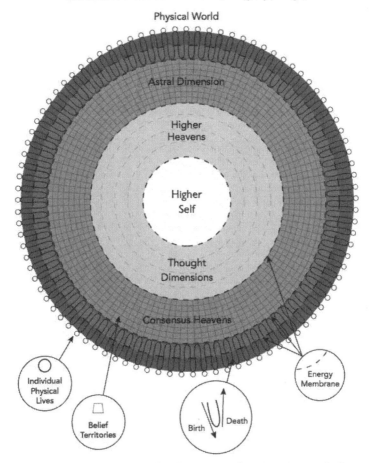

The Evolution of Consciousness/Soul through Repetitive Experiences within Form Based Realities (Bardos)

Individual learning experiences into the physical universe and back to the astral dimension (multiple journeys)

Physical World

Astral Dimension

Higher Heavens

Higher Self

Thought Dimensions

Consensus Heavens

Individual Physical Lives

Belief Territories

Birth | Death

Energy Membrane

Humans remain cloistered within the dense outer dimensions until they develop the qualities of an evolved soul. Millions of consensus realities exist created by the collective thoughts of the inhabitants.

The Intense Reality Ride of Earth

The author Robert Monroe states that reincarnating in the physical world is like repeating a wild trip on our favorite, exciting, amusement-park ride. If our goal is to break the repetitive cycle of reincarnation—or get off of the 'wheel,' as the Buddhists describe it—it is essential to awaken to our true nature. How can we ever evolve beyond matter when our complete self-identity remains focused on our physical existence. Reincarnation is a choice; it is not mandatory. No one forces us to reenter Earth, as soul, possessing free will it is always our decision. There are many conditions that continue to fuel the reincarnation process for humans. Here are the primary anchors:

1. **A false physical self-identity** – being unaware of our multidimensional spiritual nature results in our continuing focus on the physical body and the physical world.
2. **Attachments to the physical world** – this can be attachment to people, relationships, homes, and life situations.
3. **Addictions** – the growing physical and psychological addictions that plague mankind compel us to return to the physical world.
4. **Absence of self-knowledge** – we are taught from birth that the answers to our existence are unknowable and that we must rely on flawed manmade philosophies and beliefs concerning our afterlife journey.
5. **Settling** – out of ignorance many people accept the first nonphysical reality they experience immediately after death.
6. **Emotional attachments** – our continuing attachment to loved ones who have died or reincarnated.

7. **Lack of self-awareness** – remaining completely unaware of our multidimensional nature, the purpose of our life, the unseen trajectory of our evolution and how to navigate the many thought responsive realities we will experience at death.

8. **Boredom** – the driving need to relive the intense stimulation that visiting the physical world can provide.

9. **Desire for additional physical lessons** – recognizing the opportunity to gain more knowledge and experience through the many intense dramas of the physical life cycle.

A physically centered and indoctrinated mindset will drive repetitive physical life experiences and behavioral choices. The number of educational incarnations required for each individual is not important, for everyone is immortal and awakens at a different pace. Each individual soul selects and creates their personal training curriculum in all dimensions.

How to Obtain Escape Velocity (Liberation) from the Earth-Life Training System

- Awaken to the raw reality of your existence. Seek the truth; reject all forms of religious and intellectual indoctrination.

- Become aware of your multidimensional nature, for we are a microcosm of the universe, seen and unseen. The physical world is the dense epidermis of an amazing expanse of energies. Your physical body is a temporary vehicle used by our consciousness for expression in the dense training realities of Earth.

- Accumulate accurate knowledge about the universal journey of consciousness we call death. Awaken to the realization that the direct spiritual path is within you. Death is actually the shift of our awareness from our outer vehicle to our existing higher frequency energy body. Soul never dies; it simply changes the density of its outer vehicle of expression.

- Know that the reality (heaven) that most people enter after physical death is actually a thought-created consensus construct located within the astral dimension and far from our true spiritual home.

- Be aware that countless thought created realities make-up the nonphysical dimensions (heavens) or what the Buddhists refer to as the bardos. Recognize that all form-based realities in every dimension (including the physical) are impermanent projections of thought.

- To achieve escape velocity and liberation reject all limiting belief systems and focus on self-empowerment through personal spiritual experiences and exploration. You are the direct inner dimensional path to liberation.

- Fully embrace your creative abilities to create your life. No excuses, you are the creative designer of your reality in every dimension. Own it.

- Become an active explorer of consciousness through meditation, lucid dreams, OBEs, trance states, or the method that best resonates with you.

- Learn how to effectively navigate the many thought responsive environments and dimensions of the universe that dwell within you.
- Create a detailed action plan for your ideal spiritual journey at death. *(A Spiritual Directive planning document is located in the Appendix.)*
- In order to enter the higher dimensional realities our personal vibrational frequency must be equal to or in-sync with each energy environment we enter.
- Escape velocity occurs when we awaken and effectively navigate the entire inner expanse of our multidimensional self. We graduate when we consciously reunite with our spiritual source.

An Awakened Death

'Phowa' is a traditional Buddhist practice, also known as 'the transference of consciousness.' The purpose of this ceremony is to support the dying with a clear set of principles and guidance for an enlightened death. The ultimate goal is to experience liberation from the wheel of reincarnation.

It is a meditation practice involving the transformation of your mind into an enlightened one at the moment of death. By invoking or reciting the name and image of Buddha, the practitioner enters into a meditative state that merges their mind with that of the ultimate Buddha nature. The dying person dissolves into light and blends with the essence of the enlightened Buddha.

The full Phowa practice is a complicated ritual activity which ideally should be conducted by a qualified Buddhist master. This is not always practical, so I have included some affirmations and a Phowa inspired script (found in Chapter Ten) that you can use. Many Buddhists believe that performing this ceremony provides favorable conditions for liberation from the many bardos (form-based realities of the astral and physical dimension) or if it is more appropriate - a positive, productive rebirth.

Create Your Own Enlightened Transition

For two decades I have written about the need for us to become effective explorers of consciousness. It's essential that we develop our ideal state of consciousness so that we are truly prepared for the transition of consciousness we call death. As creative spiritual beings it's imperative that we take complete responsibility for our life and our continuing journey at death. With this mindset the following personal action plan is presented.

1) Create a written plan for your death. Select allies you trust who will support and assist your personal spiritual action plan. Make sure they are aware of your detailed instructions prior to the dying process: you may have limited communication ability as your transition draws near. (Refer to the Spiritual Directive document in the appendix.)

2) Release all your attachments to the physical world and your physical body. Take the actions you need to assure your state of consciousness and emotional frequency is at the highest possible point. Provide forgiveness where needed and gratitude for all that you have experienced during this physical life.

3) During the entire process of death focus your mind on your ultimate spiritual objective. Create and repeat your highest intention for an enlightened transition. Make it powerful mantra. (Spiritual Essence Now! Higher Self Now!)

4) Create a personal sacred space that reflects and supports your highest spiritual intention. Many include inspirational art, images and objects that reinforce their highest spiritual goals.

5) Create or purchase a verbal audio guidance recording of affirmations for yourself and your loved ones. These affirmations should support your specific spiritual goals. Make sure this is documented in your plan. (My audio program, _Destination: Higher Self_ was created for this purpose.)

6) Be certain your personal affirmation plan and recording is accessible to those who will assist you during the entire process. Play your personal affirmation recording at your bedside before, during and after death.

7) Cremation of the body can assist us to break any remaining attachments to the physical world and our temporary biological vehicle. Do this as quickly as possible.

Taking Spiritual Action

It is essential that we take spiritual action in order to propel our consciousness beyond the dense gravity field of the physical and the astral dimensions. The great spiritual masters throughout history were well aware of this fact. Buddha instructed us to detach from the physical world and release all the attachments and desires that bind us to matter. Jesus taught us to seek first the kingdom of God with all of our heart and our entire mind. If you examine the teachings of any spiritual master you will hear a resounding call for spiritual action. Belief and faith are only the first steps of spirituality. Granted, belief is an important first step, but religious beliefs and traditions alone were never intended to be the sole aspect of spirituality. Jesus, Buddha and other enlightened spiritual leaders never taught us to become dependent on man-made beliefs. Their lives were vibrant examples of personal spiritual action and exploration. Ask yourself this critical question: Are you content to settle for man-made traditions and beliefs, or are you ready to take the next step in your spiritual evolution?

Let us embrace a new approach to death and dying. Instead of fear, let us embrace joy, for we know that we continue to live and love beyond the dense vehicle of flesh. Our exit from this temporary training ground is a glorious return to our true spiritual home. Let us open our hearts and minds to the formless void of pure spiritual consciousness. Let us embrace the journey of death as a self-empowering launch pad propelling us to the very core of our spiritual essence. With this focused intention death becomes a powerful opportunity for us to experience liberation.

Our expanded knowledge of the thought responsive nature of the afterlife and the elimination of our fears concerning death and dying are major steps forward for all humankind. We are awakening to the fact that death is a natural transition of consciousness, a continuation of life.

Just imagine the potential benefits of an enlightened transition. You approach death with a clear awareness of your spiritual goal. You are empowered to focus on your spiritual intention. As the moment draws near, you focus on and demand to experience your highest spiritual essence, "Higher Self Now! With your ultimate goal firmly established you separate from your body and move rapidly inward through layers of energy and consciousness to the very core of your spiritual self. The possibilities are limitless, however, it is up to us be self-empowered and take positive spiritual action.

Hope and beliefs alone are not an effective spiritual plan for our transition of consciousness at death. We have the ability to break free from the institutional indoctrination and become an active explorer of consciousness during our life and at death. A pivotal shift of awareness is now occurring worldwide as millions realize that we design not only our current reality, but our afterlife as well. We are not victims at death, we are immortal spiritual beings empowered to explore, discover and experience escape velocity and liberation from the training ground of souls.

CHAPTER 9

Our Continuing Evolution after Death

"There is no death. Only a change of worlds."

CHIEF SEATTLE

The Afterlife Journey

IN THE AFTERLIFE, people of like mind are drawn together and share a collective vision of reality. Their new home will be a wonderful transition from the harsh challenges we experience in the physical world. Many of the hardships are no longer present because, as previously mentioned there is no biological decay, illness, aging, starvation, or war. At death most people blissfully accept and embrace the first nonphysical environment they experience without question and—due to a lack of knowledge—most assume that this initial destination is their heavenly home.

However, those who have acquired some level of spiritual self-knowledge while still living on Earth realize that their voyage of discovery continues after death. They know that many dimensions exist and they are aware that their journey is just beginning. Most importantly they understand that their state of awareness will determine their destination at death.

The Evolution of Soul is a Multidimensional Process

Our personal evolution is accomplished through intense individual experiences within many different energy realities. Nothing external restricts us on our spiritual path; we create our own limits and blocks by our attachments to matter, our state of consciousness and our flawed physical self-identity. Soul presents itself in a variety of biological shapes to achieve its singular goal of spiritual evolution. All life forms are but temporary vehicles used for the expression, awakening and evolution of consciousness. This is how we become empowered to truly take our place within the higher-vibrational dimensions (heavens) of our multiverse. The following are some key points to remember.

1. Everything is a manifestation of consciousness.
2. We are using three-dimensional bodies to function within various dense energy environments.
3. All the form-based realities we experience are a projection. All three-dimensional objects and realities in every dimension are essentially crystalized thought-forms.
4. Through trial and error we learn to distinguish the difference between our self-created thought-forms and the established consensus collective realities that we experience.
5. We must awaken to and develop the various inner senses that are inherent within each energy body we use. Each energy body we possess has unique perception and mobility capabilities.

6. We continue to experience our self-created thought-energy projections in the form of lessons until they are resolved. This is a multidimensional process.

7. The human concept of linear time is meaningless in our continuing evolution as soul/consciousness.

8. As we evolve we learn to effectively and consciously traverse our various energy bodies with control. This is the essential skill of a truly evolved soul.

9. As we evolve we consciously experience our spiritual essence and become a fully aware being without limits.

The Evolution of Soul/Consciousness through Extensive Experiences in Multiple Dimensions

We are all playing a multidimensional game of life; however, most humans remain aware of only a single energy level—the physical. As we learn to effectively navigate multiple energy environments, we gain the ability to accelerate our individual development and evolution. Each dimension we experience provides unique opportunities for our personal spiritual growth.

Major Stages in the Evolution of Soul

Stage 1 - The basic training ground of consciousness (Earth)
Upon entering the physical world (birth), we begin our education through intense personal experiences in the slowed-down molecular training ground of Earth. The physical world provides the ultimate energy simulations for developing consciousness. By the very process of entering matter we are extending our state of consciousness throughout the entire multidimensional spectrum

of the universe. The very act of operating a dense biological vehicle is an integral element of our training. Few humans are aware that this mind expanding extension of consciousness is a central aspect of our development and evolution. Currently all of us are in training to become fully conscious multidimensional spiritual beings. We are developing our awareness in order to enter and effectively function within the magnificent instant thought responsive realities of the higher dimensions. The basic training of Earth includes:

- Transferring and maintaining our consciousness into a temporary biological vehicle.
- Learning how to function effectively in a dense environment and to operate a biological body.
- Learning through trial and error from our intense physical challenges, dramas, and relationships.
- Seeking the answers to life-changing questions such as: What am I? What is my life's purpose? Where am I going at death? What is the nature of heaven?
- Searching for accurate knowledge about our existence as soul/consciousness.
- Researching/studying various spiritual exploration methods to still the ego mind and initiate a profound experience (meditation, breath work, mantras, yoga, etc.)
- Opening to our intuition and our nonphysical nature and capabilities.
- Purging our mind of all the ideas that slow our growth and distort our perception.
- Awakening to the realization that we create the many lessons in our life.
- Learning to exercise personal responsibility for our thoughts and actions.

- Working to eliminate our personal fears and limits as we develop our conscious awareness.
- Awakening to our multidimensional nature and our inner path of evolution.
- Developing a personal blueprint to experience an enlightened transition.
- Accepting the eventual death of our physical vehicle/ body and embracing the transfer back to the existing energy body within us.

Stage 2 - The first nonphysical reality (heaven) we experience after death
At death, most people will awaken within a nonphysical energy reality that is often assumed to be 'heaven.' This is a pleasant group consensus environment within the astral dimension. Upon death, most experience their 'physical-like astral body,' the densest of the many energy bodies we will experience as we continue our journey of consciousness. This new nonphysical environment is created by the collective thoughts of the local inhabitants. During this major stage of our afterlife journey we will experience:

- A wonderful meeting and reunification with our loved ones who inhabit the dimensional reality we have entered.
- A rest and recuperation period for those souls who have experienced a sudden and/or traumatic death.
- An orientation and assimilation into our nonphysical energy body and environment.
- Adapting to the function and capabilities of our subtle energy body and the norms of the consensus reality of which we are now a part.
- Learning to effectively communicate by thought.

- A review of what we have learned during our last adventure on Earth. How did we respond to the various challenges and dramas that we experienced? What did we learn?

A pivotal decision point in our continuing evolution

After physical death, people participate in an examination of their last adventure on Earth. This is an essential opportunity for self- appraisal and renewal. After they have reunited with loved ones most souls will consider what they have learned from their last incarnation. Depending upon the development of the individual they will begin to select the educational opportunities, life situations, interactions and parents that will best facilitate their personal spiritual development. Since linear time does not exist in nonphysical realities, this process of reentry into matter can manifest as years, decades or even centuries in physical time.

Most humans return to the physical world for additional training, however, a relatively small percentage will continue their self-development within the nonphysical dimensions. Each reality and dimension we experience provides unique educational opportunities. Our graduation from matter is just the beginning of our continuing evolution.

Stage 3 - Educational experiences within the astral dimension
are physical-like in nature and can include:

- Adapting to our initial nonphysical (astral) body and our new energy environment.
- Awakening to the provisional nature of our physical-like self-identity.

- Recognizing and reducing our fears and limits.
- Opening to the reality of our extensive nonphysical nature and our true home beyond the limits of matter.
- Remembering our authentic self and our primary educational mission for visiting Earth.
- Determining the aspects of our development that require further attention, and forming a strategy to proceed.
- Seeking out guides and teachers who can assist us in the exploration of our multidimensional nature and help us to define the next steps on our spiritual path.
- Becoming aware that other energy dimensions and environments exist beyond the first nonphysical reality (heaven).
- Acknowledging our unlimited creative capabilities.
- Learning to effectively experience and explore other realities beyond our initial environment.
- Discovering how to transcend our current energy body.

Stage 4 - The next inner dimensional training environments
Next we enter the higher-vibrational (less dense, more thought-responsive) energy level within the astral dimension. This is sometimes called the 'second death' because the initial astral body is shed. This training area will incorporate:

- Adapting to our higher-vibrational energy body and its enhanced capabilities.
- Exploring our new vibrational energy environment and acclimating to its increased thought-responsive nature.
- Awakening to the presence of a mentor or guide to assist us in our continuing education and training.
- Cleansing our astral body of the fears, blocks, and limiting emotional patterns and subconscious drives we

continue to hold. This training is achieved through various energy simulations. This educational process is detailed in <u>Adventures in the Afterlife</u>.

- Developing our subtle inner senses and the full creative potential of our new energy body.
- Learning the essential navigation and control skills needed to enter multiple astral realities.
- Exploring the many environments of the astral dimension. Becoming aware of the heavens/belief territories that populate this dimension.
- Navigating the diverse nonphysical realities of the astral dimension and learning to function effectively in consensus, non-consensus, and void environments.

Stage 5 - The progressively higher-vibrational training realities
As we continue to explore inner (less dense) higher-vibrational nonphysical energy levels, we begin to awaken to the educational purpose of all form-based realities. We are learning to effectively control the immense creative energies of our thoughts. This training will include:

- Transcending the limits of our astral body and becoming more aware of our higher-frequency thought-energy body.
- Energetically entering and exploring ever-higher inner energy levels of the nonphysical dimensions.
- Adapting to our higher-vibrational (less dense) energy body and its enhanced capabilities.
- Learning to effectively maneuver in different types of thought-responsive realities. This can include consensus, non-consensus, and voids.

- Developing the mindset that we are the creative force responsible for shaping our reality in all dimensions.
- Practicing complete responsibility for all of our thoughts and actions.
- Learning the art and practice of energy and frequency manifestation.
- Discovering various methods of exploration to expand beyond the limits of a single energy body.
- Clearing each inner energy body of all negative energies (fears and limits) and attachments to form and density.
- Becoming a guide, healer, or teacher to assist the local inhabitants. Supporting others in their spiritual education.
- Making the decision to accept this energy space as home or to continue our exploration into even higher-vibrational dimensions.

Stage 6 - The advanced training realities of the thought-based dimensions
Eventually we begin adapting to and becoming familiar with the creative capabilities of our mental body and the corresponding thought-responsive dimensional realities. Our mental body is essentially our thought-based energy vehicle and is significantly less dense than our astral body. This body is energetically closer in frequency to our essence and has greater creative potential and freedom than the astral vehicle of consciousness. This educational stage involves:

- Entering and adapting to the higher-frequency thought-responsive dimensions.

- Learning to exercise complete responsibility and control over all of our thought projections.
- Studying how to create and manipulate form-based realities.
- Understanding how to effectively function in an immense spectrum of thought-responsive environments.
- Discovering how to manifest and manipulate energies within the denser dimensions.
- Becoming aware of an advanced guide or mentor to assist us in our development.
- Cleansing our mental body of our fears, limits, or other restrictive energies or thoughts.
- Becoming a guide, healer, or teacher to assist the local inhabitants. Assisting others in their spiritual awakening and education.

Stage 7 - Mastering our multidimensional creative capabilities
As we gain an understanding of our unlimited creative abilities in all dimensions, we are learning to skillfully navigate in all instant thought-responsive realities—the higher heavens. This development includes:

- Directing the enormous creative capabilities of our mental (thought) body.
- Acquiring complete control over all our thought projections.
- Learning to enter and experience the realities of the mental dimension.
- Mastering the art and practice of creation within all the dimensional realities of thought and form.
- Awakening to the knowledge that even our mind is a temporary vehicle of our soul/consciousness.

- Continuing our journey beyond the mind and thought.
- Connecting with and experiencing our higher self.
- Becoming an advanced guide or teacher to assist others in their awakening.

Stage 8 - Becoming a fully aware, spiritually evolved, multidimensional being

The truly evolved soul becomes fully aware of their unlimited ability to experience the entire expanse of their multidimensional self and the multiverse. At this advanced level of evolution we will:

- Exercise complete creative control over our entire multidimensional self, our thought projections, and all the energy environments we experience.
- Emanate unconditional love to all beings.
- Perfect the ability to move our conscious awareness through all of our energy bodies (vehicles of expression) within every level of the universe.
- Master our capacity for controlled exploration through all dimensions and realities.
- Become an advanced interdimensional traveler without limits.
- Use our creative abilities to manipulate and control the diverse energies and frequencies of the universe for the good of all sentient beings.
- Experience complete freedom of mobility in all dimensional realities.
- Become a highly advanced spiritual guide, teacher, or master to assist in the progress of all souls.
- Be a fully conscious, multidimensional master of all energies and realities.

- Experience the multidimensional totality of our higher self.
- Extend and control our conscious awareness beyond all form-based concepts and realities.
- Transcend all concepts of linear time and space.
- Experience unity with the spiritual source of all creation.
- Evolve beyond all existing human and form-based concepts.

Our death is just the beginning: we continue our journey of consciousness and eventually reunite with our spiritual essence beyond the dense outer dimensions of form. There are no limits or end points to how we awaken. Because we are all immortal, the length of time and the number of incarnations within every dimension is meaningless. Embrace the expanded freedom and awareness that comes from becoming an active explorer of consciousness.

Special Note - Awaken to your Continuing Journey

If immediately after your death, you find yourself in a pleasant physical-like reflection of your past Earth environment, you are now standing within the astral dimension and far from your true spiritual home. Recognize that your journey has just begun and that you possess the creative ability to enhance your state of awareness and your resulting afterlife reality. You are an immortal spiritual being without limits; never settle for the mundane. Awaken! Your focused thoughts and intentions possess immeasurable creative power. Remember to, *own your creative power.* Repeat your highest intention and aim for your ultimate spiritual goal - Higher Self Now!

CHAPTER 10

Techniques to Support Awakening

"It's only when we truly know and understand that we have a limited time on Earth and that we have no way of knowing when our time is up, we will begin to live each day to the fullest as if it was the only one we had."

ELIZABETH KUBLER-ROSS

NOW IS THE time to focus on some actions that will support your transition at the highest possible level. In this chapter, I will share some techniques, affirmations, and practices that will strengthen your daily spiritual life and prepare you for the transition from the physical to the nonphysical.

Create Your Highest Spiritual Intention

Take the time necessary to determine your ultimate spiritual intention. Meditate upon this single question: what is the ultimate spiritual goal for your life? Is it self-awareness? Enlightenment? Conscious union with your spiritual source? Liberation? Use the terms that best clarify your highest personal intention. Make this your focused goal.

A boat without a rudder will drift and founder in the ocean. By setting our life's course we begin to navigate our journey and accelerate our growth. One easy method of directing our intention is to create a clear affirmation and repeat it several times a day, like a mantra. For example, repeating "Higher self now" or "Spiritual essence now" can be powerful. Do this for several days and notice any vibrational changes or shifts of perception occurring in your state of consciousness. Often, your entire being may feel lighter and brighter. Repeating your mantra as you drift to sleep can also initiate lucid dreams and OBEs. Hold your intention as your last thought when you drift to sleep.

Carve Your Primary Spiritual Intention into your Mind

Close your eyes and become centered. Calm your mind and visualize a large block of stone or marble; this stone represents your subconscious mind. Imagine carving your focused intention into the stone. Use the present tense; for example, "Spiritual Essence Now! Higher Self Now!" Clearly imagine carving each letter and word with a chisel or power tool. Feel it manifesting. Touch it. Make it absolutely real with the unlimited power of your mind. Step back and observe your creation. See, sense, or feel it clearly. Acknowledge that you have just carved your primary goal into your mind. Absolutely accept and know that your highest spiritual intention has become a permanent part of your conscious and subconscious mind. Now accept and embrace your spiritual intention as an essential part of your complete being. Repeat this visualization until it becomes second nature to you. Do this daily and preferably before your meditation and all exploration of consciousness sessions.

SCRIPTS AND NOTES FOR TECHNIQUES AND GUIDED VISUALIZATIONS

In the following section you will find scripts, visualizations and techniques, some of which are used during my workshops at The Monroe Institute. I suggest that you record your own voice (or that of someone you know) with soft music in the background. Hemi-Sync® is an ideal support system for these techniques. The following exercises may assist you in clearing the path to your higher self. Select one or more of these that resonate with you and incorporate them into your daily spiritual practices.

WATERFALL

This is a cleansing technique that may assist you to clear your mind of any active emotions, social dramas, or self-imposed limitations so that you can better absorb the techniques listed below.

Focus on your breathing and with every breath you can feel yourself relaxing deeper and deeper.

As you let go and flow you can see before you a beautiful cleansing waterfall.

As you approach the waterfall you can feel the tremendous energy radiating from it.

You can feel that this waterfall will cleanse and purify your entire body and mind, it will saturate every aspect of your conscious and subconscious mind and dissolve away all fears and limits from your entire energy field.

Now feel that you are moving gently forward into the waterfall. Feel the cleansing power as it saturates every cell and system of your body and mind.

You can feel the calming liquid cleansing your conscious and subconscious mind.

It is gently flowing down your face and shoulders relaxing every cell, every tissue.

You can feel all of your limits and blocks being dissolved away. See and feel this now.

And you can feel yourself becoming lighter and lighter as all heaviness is being washed away.

This cleansing water saturates every corner of your conscious and subconscious mind washing away all of your fears and limits.

You can sense and feel this now. You can feel yourself becoming lighter and lighter and you know you are always protected when you explore beyond your physical limits.

Take a moment to see and feel this happening. You are becoming cleansed. You feel lighter and lighter.

Surrender to this powerful healing liquid. Allow all limits and blocks to be washed away.

BUILDING A BRIDGE TO YOUR HIGHER SELF

This technique is designed to help you manifest a conscious connection with your higher self by creating a visual bridge from your physical state of consciousness to your spiritual essence.

Take several deep breaths and allow yourself to relax completely. Bring your full awareness to the top of your head.

Use the unlimited power of your mind and imagine that there are two beautiful green islands separated by a river. One island represents your conscious mind and the other is your Higher Self.

Clearly imagine that you are constructing a solid bridge between these two islands, these two parts of your being. Take a few moments and vividly see and feel that you are constructing your personal bridge that connects the two islands.

This bridge can be any shape or form that you focus on, for you are the designer and the builder.

Take a few moments and feel this bridge taking form and becoming a permanent part of you. Focus all of your senses to create a solid structure. (Take the time you need to visualize the bridge.)

You can clearly perceive this bridge now, connecting the two islands, the two parts of your being. And now at your own pace you can feel and sense yourself moving across your bridge. You are gliding effortlessly over the bridge. From now on you have the ability to access and remember your experiences with greater and greater clarity.

All limits and blocks dissolve away.

Vividly see yourself effortlessly moving over the bridge to the other island. You can feel the freedom and know that you are welcome. You feel completely at home.

From now on you will vividly feel and sense the inner connection and communication with your spiritual essence.

You can feel yourself opening to the unlimited knowledge and unconditional love of your spiritual self.

Take a moment to acknowledge that you have created a permanent bridge between your conscious mind and your higher self. Feel the inner connection.

From now on you are open to connect with your higher self in full waking consciousness. You can easily create a solid connection to your higher self.

You absolutely sense and feel this inner connection between your conscious mind and your spiritual essence. You accept this connection with every level of your body and mind. From this moment on, you are able to access your higher self with greater and greater clarity.

DOORWAYS OF LIGHT

This technique will allow you to give and accept forgiveness, separate from attachments that bind you to the physical, and move into an environment that supports the transition to your higher self.

Breathe deeply and relax completely.

All thoughts dissolve as your spinal column is glowing with warm, loving light.

The light fills your body until your entire being is glowing with bright white light. You feel lighter and lighter.

Now use the unlimited power of your mind and imagine, feel, or sense that a glowing doorway appears before you. Take a moment, and know that this special door is just for you. This door opens the pathway to your spiritual essence…your higher self.

As you move closer to the door, you can see a personal message carved into the door.

Forgiveness Now.

Repeat this in your mind and allow it to become one with you.

Forgiveness Now.

This phrase is bold and powerful.

You consider all those who ask for your forgiveness and you easily give it.

Feel this happening as you become lighter and lighter. You clearly forgive yourself and all others for any event that may have occurred in your life.

You think to yourself: I forgive and release all...and all forgive and release me... Take a moment and surrender to forgiveness...feel this happening now as you step through the door.

Through every level of your body and mind, you acknowledge that all is forgiven

Appearing before you is another glowing door. Boldly carved into the door are two words.

Detachment Now.

Repeat this in your mind and allow it to become one with you.

Detachment Now.

This is bold and powerful.

Allow all physical and emotional issues to dissolve away, and you become lighter and lighter. As you surrender all attachments, the door easily opens and you pass through. Take a moment and release all attachments to matter and form.

A deep sense of freedom saturates your being as all attachments to density melt away.

Now beyond the door, you can see or sense that you are again gliding along a bright hallway of radiant light. Moving inward to your spiritual essence, you approach another glowing door before you.

Moving closer, you examine the details of this door where you can see a clear message. Boldly engraved on the door is the phrase:

Higher Self Now!

All heaviness dissolves as you saturate your mind with your focused spiritual intention.

Now I merge with my higher self!

Reaching out, you open and step through the doorway marked 'Higher Self.' Your ability to experience your spiritual essence becomes greater and greater.

As you move through this door, you realize that you have entered a bright new reality and you are floating in a glowing vaulted chamber of pure radiant light. You feel empowered, lighter and lighter.

You know that from now on, all doors to your spiritual source open effortlessly for you.

Your focused intention, *Higher Self Now* is now etched into your conscious and subconscious mind.

All attachments to form dissolve and you surrender to your spiritual essence.

Lighter and lighter…floating free…focusing on your intention.

You acknowledge that all doors to your higher self are open for you…you are now empowered to experience your spiritual source…you are now empowered to achieve liberation.

Lighter and lighter you float upward into a vast sea of pure white light. Surrender and feel this happening, floating, reuniting with the clear light of your essence.

Focus and repeat your highest intention, *Higher Self Now!*

BALLOON TECHNIQUE

This method is intended to assist you as you release all the baggage and issues in your life that are blocking you from having a profound spiritual experience.

Breathe deeply and relax completely. With each exhale you can feel all tension dissolving away.

It's a warm summer's day and you are walking along a path through a green field. You can see mountains in the background. Clearly imagine a beautiful green field before you.

With every step along the path, you feel yourself becoming more and more relaxed and at ease.

In the distance at the bottom of a hill, you can clearly sense or see that there is an impressive hot air balloon ready to launch. This balloon can be any color that you choose. Take a moment and imagine the details of this hot air balloon before you.

As you move closer to the balloon, you can begin to see the details of the gondola. The balloon is ready to launch and you can clearly see that four ropes are holding it to the earth.

As you move closer, you can touch the texture of the gondola and you can sense yourself entering the basket of the balloon. Your energy body is light as a feather. You are now inside of the gondola and looking out onto the green field around you.

Your balloon is ready to launch and you are ready to fly. Four ropes are holding the balloon down and each one symbolizes any fears, limits, or blocks you now hold. As you cut the ropes, you are cutting all of your attachments to form. One by one, you cut the anchors and watch as they fall away. All attachments to your body fall away. With each cut you are releasing yourself from all energy blocks and attachments.

As you release your connection to the ground, the balloon rises gently upward. Slowly up at first, and then more quickly. You are weightless and rising upward.

You look below and see the rolling green hills as you watch as the houses below become smaller and smaller. The trees and buildings appear smaller as you move effortlessly, higher and higher, through the sky.

Now look over your right shoulder to see a guide who is helping to direct the balloon. You can ask any question that you would like. You will gain clear insights to anything that is on your mind. Now take a moment and ask a question.

Continue to rise and glide above the rolling hills. You are moving higher and higher, higher and higher - away from the earth. You are over 1000 feet high when you feel yourself slowing down. You are no longer gliding as quickly when you notice that there are bags of sand attached to the side of your basket. This extra weight has slowed your movement. These bags represent all your attachments, fears, limits, and blocks. You have the ability to release all of your personal baggage and continue your journey. One at a time, you pick up the heavy baggage and drop them to the ground. You want to go higher and higher, so you release another bag and watch it plummet to the ground far below. Now you go even higher, drop another bag, watch it fall to the earth. You have now eliminated all the fears and limits that have been holding you back.

Take a moment and examine your mind. Are there any more bags of limits or fears to discard? Is there anything else keeping you from reaching your spiritual self?

Now you release all of the limits that slow your journey of consciousness; take a moment and sense and that you are free to contact your higher self.

You are lighter and lighter as you move higher and higher.

You are now moving beyond your body, traveling, opening to energies and motion.

Hold your intention as your last thought; now you have a conscious connection with your spiritual essence.

You remain aware as your body and mind drift higher.
Let go and flow with vibrations and the sound.
Let go and flow to your higher self.

REMEMBERING YOUR MISSION

This visualization is designed to help you rediscover your purpose in this physical life and to identify and thank those in your life who may be assisting you with this mission.

Breathe deeply and relax completely. With each exhale feel all tension dissolve away.

As you relax, you feel the presence of another close to you. You easily recognize this being as your spiritual guide. You are pleased to see that your guide has chosen this time to meet with you. You have many questions. These concerns are floating around you. Your companion smiles and assures you that you are on the right path. You have chosen your own way and that is essential to your evolution. You are comfortable in that knowledge.

As you continue to relax and enjoy the company of your advisor, you are given a box. It is beautiful and smooth to the touch. Colors softly move through the box and onto your hands. You notice a lid that beckons you to open it. Your guide nods, giving approval.

With one hand you remove the lid and out floats a word. This is your word. It has meaning only to you. This is your mission in the physical world. You take the word and allow it to run through your mind freely, easily. Attach this word to a situation that currently concerns you. See the faces of those who are in this scenario. You know who they are and what roles they play. You recognize that no matter what is happening, they are here to support your journey. They are the players in your life, the ones who will assist you to learn and provide help to you as you grow.

See yourself with this support group as you all play your roles, helping, guiding, and encouraging each other. Embrace your team, knowing that any unpleasant moments were placed in your life to strengthen you and bring you closer to your higher self. Thank them for all they have done, for these are the souls who have followed you as you work to achieve your mission.

At this time take a few moments to think about how you can use this information to become more connected to your higher self.

You are comfortable knowing that the path you have chosen is the right one. Now release the box, allow it to float away, knowing that you can call it back at any time for more clarity and other information. Keep the word that symbolizes your mission and allow it to be your friend. Send love and gratitude to the people who have been there during your lessons providing the obstacles and opportunities that gave you courage and strength.

Thank your guide for providing this valuable insight to you.

HEALING TECHNIQUE

This technique can be used to address both emotional and physical wounds. This is important because a high frequency emotional mindset and a functioning physical body can help to support learning and teaching opportunities in the physical world.

Breathe deeply and relax completely. With each exhale, feel all tension dissolve away.

Now, see an aura of white light surrounding your body. The light is warm and protective around you. You feel comfortable and safe with this light. It is peaceful and calming. You feel so at ease that you begin to allow the light to enter your body. Now it is flowing around you and gently moving into your body, warming you, surrounding you with love and peace. The light has moved into your skin, gently massaging any tension away. You welcome the light as it moves into your muscles, soothing any tightness. You can feel it warming your bones, and your entire body is now loose and relaxed.

As you enjoy the restful warmth of this light, you notice that there is a spot of darkness in your body, a place that will not absorb this light. You focus on this area and identify the source of the darkness. You see the cause, you know what it is. It is an area of pain or sadness. And you know you are strong enough to remove this sorrow from your physical body, restoring it to the full light-filled being that you know you can be. Forgive and release the pain. Wrap the area in love, sending your light into the place where it has been lost.

You can see the dark area being filled with light now; your love has illuminated all of your body and mind. Imagine now that your hands are up and rising above the cells that need your love. Your palms are open and facing the area. Address those cells, tell them that you love them, and see the healing light coming from your palms. Thank them for providing this learning opportunity for you; encourage these cells to light up on their own—one by one they are creating a cluster of beautiful stars. These stars fill your entire being with pleasant, warm love.

Allow a message from your Higher Self to enter your mind and body.

You can feel safe and loved knowing that this light is working on your behalf every moment of every day to comfort your body and ease your mind. The clusters of warm, soothing light will always be there for you to call on whenever you feel the need. Thank the light, love yourself.

DESTINATION: HIGHER SELF

These affirmations can be spoken out loud or recorded and played at your bedside during the end-of-life process and for some period of time after physical death has occurred. Select the phrases that are appropriate to meet your needs or those of a loved one.

With each breath, imagine and feel relaxing white light filling your body and mind.

Pure radiant light fills your awareness, and with each breath, you feel lighter and lighter...weightless...letting go... floating.

Surrender and flow with the waves as you focus on your highest spiritual intention.

With each wave you are...becoming lighter and lighter...at peace, surrounded by an ocean of love and light.

Feel the inner motion, and with each wave, let go and flow to your spiritual source...your higher self.

As you gently float in an ocean of white calming light, allow each affirmation to soak into your awareness:

Pure light and love saturate my entire being.

Waves of love and light open my awareness, as all attachments to density and form melt away.

With each wave I remember and focus on my highest spiritual intention.

Floating in an ocean of radiant white light, I am free from all density and form.

Light and love fills my mind.

I am comfortable and at peace.

Pure light and love saturate my entire being and I am lighter and lighter.

I remain focused on my highest spiritual intention.

Now I experience my higher self.

Higher Self Now!

I am my pure spiritual essence, completely loved and accepted.

I am grateful to all of my teachers in this life.

I am safe and filled with peace.

I remember and repeat my highest spiritual intention. Higher self now!

I forgive all. I release all.

Now I enter the radiant clear light, beyond all the illusions of form

I am open to unlimited love.

I feel waves of gratitude for all the love and lessons in my life.

I forgive all. I release all.

Now I am empowered to experience my higher self.

I am loved, I am love.

Awareness now! Spiritual Liberation Now! Higher Self Now!

SELF-REFLECTION

The term 'Naikan' is Japanese for inside looking, or as we would define it, self-reflection. This process was developed by Yoshimo Ishin (1916-1988). He was a devout Jodo Shinsin Buddhist who began his inner journey with sensory deprivation, confining himself to a dark cave with no food, water, or sleep. Realizing that to benefit the general public this would have to be something most people could do independently, he later introduced a more user-friendly process of digging into one's psyche. Modern practitioners in Japan say this method helps people to understand themselves and their relationships. There are three basics to consider when beginning this process:

1. Set aside a dedicated time to commit yourself to the practice.
2. Identify an isolated space that is dark, secluded, and free of distractions.
3. Use a structured application of questions that only you can answer.

Once you have defined the time that consistently works for you and a space that fits the privacy standards, the questions you must consider are as follows:

1. What have I received from _____?
2. What have I given to _____?
3. What troubles and difficulties have I caused to_____?

Today, Japan has dozens of Naikan Therapy centers that use this simple process over the course of days to uncover the root causes of everything from behavioral issues to medical concerns. It has been successful in mental health counseling and prisoner rehabilitation as well as in schools and business. This might be an appropriate place for you to begin in your quest to identify and resolve any open issues that may hinder your personal spiritual progress.

A Phowa-Inspired Technique

This technique is based on the Buddhist teachings of Phowa. See Chapter Eight for more information on the philosophy of Phowa and related practices.

Breathe deeply and relax completely.

With each exhale you drift deeper and deeper into an ideal relaxed state.

Lighter and lighter, floating gently, letting go of all thought.

Focus on your crown chakra and imagine and feel a pure clear light flowing down from above and entering the top of your head. Now feel the top of your head opening to accept this streaming light. You are lighter and lighter.

Looking up, invoke the image of a powerful spiritual being to be present with you in your experience. Choose the divine image that you feel closest to—whether it is Buddha, Jesus, or angels—or imagine a pure golden light filling the entire space around you.

Consider this the embodiment of all truth, wisdom, and compassion. See this as all Buddhas, saints, masters, and enlightened beings. Fill your heart with their presence and trust that they are here now to assist you.

Focus on the light and repeat this intention or prayer to yourself:

Through blessing, grace, and guidance, through the power of the light, may all my negative karma, destructive emotions, and blockages be purified and removed.
May I know that I am forgiven for all the harm that I may have thought and done in my life.
May I accomplish this profound practice of Phowa and die a good and peaceful death, and through the triumph of my death, may I be able to benefit all conscious beings, living and dead.

Now imagine that the presence of pure light is so moved by your sincere and heartfelt prayer that the response is a loving smile—sending out love and compassion in a stream of light from the heart.

As love touches and penetrates you, you are cleansed and purified of all your negative karma and any destructive emotions that have caused you suffering.

You now see, feel, and sense that you are totally immersed in purifying clear light. Make it so.

You are completely purified and healed by the streaming light. Your very body itself dissolves into this light.

The body of light you have now become soars up into the sky and merges with the blissful presence of life.

Now you are the clear light, soaring free, liberated from all form and the wheel of rebirth.

Be the light. Let go and flow.

HO'OPONOPONO

'Huna' is the art and science of healing and spiritual development originating in ancient Hawaii. Part of this custom is 'Ho'oponopono,' the Hawaiian code of forgiveness. This is the process of 'making it right' with the ancestors of those with whom you've had relationships. It is based on the premise that we are all connected to the Divine Consciousness and that we are all responsible for everything in our life. Once we accept that principle, then we can work to change whatever is not going well. By using this practice you can break old family patterns, relieve others of guilt, and correct any wrongs done across time. You can even forgive yourself for missing a goal in life, excessive behaviors, or doing harm to another.

You may bring up all persons across all lifetimes that you wish to acknowledge and forgive. Recite these four statements two to three times. Feel free to add any specifics that would provide more meaning to you and your situation.

- I'm sorry.
- Please forgive me.
- Thank you.
- I love you.

A VISUALIZATION TO COMPLEMENT THE HUNA TRADITION

Sit in a quiet, comfortable place with your posture in alignment. Close your eyes and take a few deep, cleansing breaths. Clear your mind of any concerns of the day. Use each breath to wash away any rambling thoughts.

Bring to mind any person or situation that has hurt you or others. Think deeply and select an intention that will serve to bring peace to your heart.

In your imagination, picture this person or situation as a heavy bottle of thick, dark fluid. You must carry it with you wherever you go. Feel the heaviness of this vessel. Look into the murky liquid and acknowledge the gloom that lies within.

Now relax even more and see yourself at your favorite location—maybe a warm sandy beach or nature trail in your local park. Perhaps you are in the city admiring the skyline or on a country farm breathing in the aroma of freshly gathered hay. But wherever you go, you must carry the heavy bottle of fluid. Walk for a while with this weight; feel how it pulls your arms down. Feel the strain in your neck as you become bent over carrying the weight of this burden. It is difficult to continue walking as your breath becomes labored and your arms and shoulders ache from the struggle.

You can no longer continue so you stop for just a moment. Suddenly a brilliant light is coming from above, surrounding you and warming your tired muscles. This is an infinite fountain of love and healing that flows from a source above the top of your head. You open your crown chakra and let the beam of love and healing flow down deep inside your body, filling you with a mysterious feeling of peace.

Now look back down at the bottle that you are carrying. It is still heavy and still dark. It is the only thing that stands in the way of your wonderfully peaceful day.

Bring back into your imagination the person or situation from your earlier thought. Ask if you have permission to send healing to them, to share the love and light that you feel.

Use these four statements with sincerity as many times as you need:

I'm sorry.
Please forgive me.
Thank you.
I love you.

As the words are spoken, the container becomes lighter and lighter. The heavy dark liquid begins to drain away.

I'm sorry.
Please forgive me.
Thank you.
I love you.

The dense glass container becomes a carefree bubble. It's light and playful. You drop it to the ground and it pops, exploding into a beautiful array of color and sparkle. The weight is lifted. Your back straightens and your shoulders relax.

I'm sorry.
Please forgive me.
Thank you.
I love you.

Now picture the person one more time and see how translucent they have become; it looks quite elegant to you. Those many shades of color mixed with the glistening light that is coming from your gaze transforms them into an enchanting sight.

There is no more pain, no more distrust or anger—only grace and warmth. Wave to them and smile; watch for them to return your greeting.

There is no limit to how many times this can be done or the number of situations that can be addressed. If you can see them or think of them without any negative emotions, then you have completed the process.

Releasing Addictions and Attachments

Many people carry their attachments to the physical world along with them at transition. This is a good time to examine your lifestyle and determine what will support a strong connection to your higher self and what might hold you closer to the physical plane. Susan told me this story about one of the guests at a hospice facility:

> *A nurse asked me to sit outside with Bonnie while she smoked a cigarette because last time there had been an accident. So of course I went out to the patio to help. She could barely hold the cigarette, her hands were so shaky. As a matter of fact, she dropped it several times while we chatted. (That seemed to be the reason for the previous "accident.") She finished that one and agreed to another. I had to pick it up from the ground after each inhale. I placed it back in her nicotine stained hands and talked about her childhood growing up on a farm in rural Maryland. I wondered later about the power of addiction. Based on her raspy voice cough, I assumed that smoking was a contributor to her premature death. She was probably not too much older than me, but it was difficult to estimate.*

When she reaches heaven, I picture her first words. "Anybody got a light?"

Where do you want to be when you wake beyond the physical? Think about anything you do that would be difficult or even impossible to release when you die. The next visualization will provide a method for you to recognize and remove any addictions that might be blocking your path.

CLEARING THE PATH

This guided visualization can be used at any time. The purpose is to let go of those things that will bind you to the physical during the transition.

It's a warm sunny day and you are happy to be walking along a natural path, one that is in your favorite park. With each step you can feel your shoes brush against the dirt and hear small crunches as you hit some leaves or twigs. You take a deep, cleansing breath; everything feels right to you. A gentle breeze hits your face and you continue to walk. There are beautiful trees on either side of the path with alternating cool shade and warm sun poking through the branches.

Ahead you can see that the sun is shining brighter and you know that's where you want to be. You pick up the pace a little bit to be closer to the brightness. Birds are singing, squirrels are chasing each other around the trees, and you have never been more content and comfortable. You even close your eyes for a moment as you continue to walk so you can appreciate the smells and sounds around you. Just walking, gentle breezes, the lyrical whistle of the birds, and then your foot hits something and you have to stop.

Before you there is a huge boulder that completely blocks your path. There is no way around it. It is too tall to climb. It's too heavy to push. You know that this boulder represents something that blocks your progress. You know what it is. Think about what it represents to you. It ties you to this place and it keeps you from going any farther on your path. The sky is becoming darker as this boulder blocks the warm sun that you saw farther ahead. It is powerful, heavy, and cold. You sit on the ground and lean against the boulder, wondering what you can do to continue your journey.

A butterfly lands on your shoulder and you hear a calming voice in your ear. "You have given away your power by attaching yourself to this barrier. You are more than your physical desires. You are a mighty spiritual being. Let nothing stand in your way." You realize that the only thing stopping you from your destination is your own self-doubt. "You are more than your physical desires," repeats the butterfly. "You know you can do it." Following the lead of that voice, you stand up and push at the boulder, lightly at first, but then you give it a hard shove. It breaks into tiny pebbles and dust. Your path is no longer blocked.

The light ahead is once again bright and warm, the trail is open, and you continue to walk confidently toward the beautiful glowing light. The soft voice once again reminds you, "You are a powerful spiritual being. Let nothing stop you from becoming your higher self."

Grounding

After any technique, it's important to journal the thoughts or experiences that you remember. Once you have completed your documentation, it is wise to ground yourself before you resume your normal activity; this especially applies to driving a vehicle immediately after any altered-state experience. Here are a few basic methods that are used today:

1. Participate in any physical activity, walking, exercise, eating etc.
2. Spend time in nature. If possible walk barefoot, connecting your feet to the earth. Run your hands along a shrub or the bark of a tree. Feel your connection with the earth.
3. While seated or standing in a comfortable position, imagine that your spinal column is a tree growing or expanding its roots into the ground and securing you to the earth.

When you regain your feelings of physical presence, you can continue to enjoy the stillness with peace of mind. Your state of relaxation can continue, and your mind will be more centered on the physical.

CHAPTER 11

❧

Navigating Nonphysical States of Consciousness

"Until you make the unconscious conscious, it will direct your life and you will call it fate."

C. G. JUNG

A Guide for the Exploration of Consciousness

BASED ON EXPERIENCE, I've found that the more prepared we are for our explorations of consciousness the more effective we can become. With knowledge we can master consensus, non-consensus and void environments with increasing levels of skill and confidence.

Our physical concepts have little bearing within the nonphysical dimensions of the universe. To become effective explorers we must learn the nonphysical 'rules of the road.' To assist your explorations, I have detailed an overview of commonly reported situations, events, and challenges. This trouble shooting guide is the result of four decades of personal experience and feedback that I've received from thousands of people who have explored various altered states of consciousness, lucid dreams and OBEs.

Remember, everything is a manifestation of consciousness; every three-dimensional form is a projection of consciousness. We are the creative center of our experiences and we must learn to take complete responsibility for our thought-energy projections within every energy level of the universe. Each challenge we confront and resolve is orchestrated to provide opportunities for us to enhance of our state of consciousness. This knowledge is critical in all our experiences and within all dimensions.

What occurs during Explorations of Consciousness?

Out-of-Body experiences, Near Death experiences, and even death itself are all the same basic inner shift of consciousness from the outer epidermis of matter to the unseen dimensions of our vast unseen multiverse. During all explorations of consciousness the only reality that appears solid to us is the one in that is in-sync with the vibrational frequency of our current energy body. Be aware, as we move or phase our consciousness inwardly beyond the physical, the perception of our surroundings will change in accordance to our state of consciousness. For the first decade of my OBEs this dramatic environment change was often disorienting. I quickly learned that the established concept of a single stable energy reality is a completely false conclusion. Multiple energy dimensions and realities coexist with us now. The various dimensions are separated by their individual vibrational frequency and resulting density.

The clearest description of our multiverse is a series of energy levels that become progressively less dense as we explore inward toward the universal energy source. Each inner, less dense, dimension serves as the supporting energy substructure for the outer one, creating a cohesive and structured continuum. All dimensions exist simultaneously and we exist as a living microcosm of this amazing multidimensional projection of consciousness. These unseen dimensions were called heaven or paradise by the early mystics and prophets who wrote the Bible, the Koran and other revered texts; a fitting description given the radiant beauty of many of these thought responsive realities.

In subtle nonphysical realities the results of our thoughts can manifest rapidly. As explorers we must be prepared for rapid shifts of consciousness and the reality changes that will result. As we raise our internal vibration we are essentially moving our conscious awareness inward. As this occurs your current "solid" reality will often appear to quickly melt or morph before you. Your state of consciousness will always determine your perceived reality. As you enhance your vibrational frequency through affirmations such as, "Clarity Now, Awareness Now, or Next Level Now!" you will energetically begin to move your awareness inward to your multidimensional self. This ability to comprehend, adjust and ultimately control our state of consciousness is critical to effectively explore the universe within us. Stay calm during all inner dimensional shifts of awareness and if required silently demand, "Stability Now!" to stabilize any oscillating state of consciousness within a specific altered state experience. The core of spiritual self-empowerment is the knowing that you are the creative force of your experience in every dimension.

The purpose of this information is to provide clear guidance to successfully maneuver during the exploration of consciousness and when entering thought-responsive environments. Accurate knowledge is essential to navigate the many projections of thought that dominate the various realities in all dimensions. It's vital that we become proficient multidimensional explorers or risk becoming pawns of the many belief systems and group consensus realities that dominate the physical and nonphysical worlds. Remember, thoughts shape and mold reality in every dimension and every form-based construct is a temporary projection of consciousness. Embrace your personal creative power and remain calm and focused during all shifts of consciousness. All control commands such as, "Awareness Now" should be powerful focused demands with the expectation of an immediate result.

Navigating the Multidimensional Labyrinth of Consciousness

The following information can be useful during all explorations of consciousness; deep meditation, lucid dreams, OBEs, shamanic and plant medicine journeys, etc.

- **The perception or sensation of rapid inner or upward motion of your awareness. The experience of being drawn into unknown nonphysical areas of yourself.**

This is our mind's interpretation of an inner shift of consciousness, often from one energy body to another within us; the expansion or movement of our awareness from one energy (frequency) level to another. This perception of inner motion is often intense and can be startling if you are not prepared. You are shifting your awareness inwardly from one energy body to a finer-frequency energy vehicle existing within yourself. This is an essential and positive expansion. Remain calm and surrender to the motion, then stabilize your awareness with a firm command. "Focus now!"

- **Catalepsy or sleep paralysis. The inability to move your body during sleep or any altered state or meditative state of consciousness.**

Remain calm, for this is a normal phenomenon that often occurs during a trance, altered states of consciousness and OBEs. Our higher-frequency energy body is temporarily out of phase with our physical body. This is a positive indication of your inner progress. Focus and maintain your awareness away from your physical body to enhance your inner exploration or to initiate an OBE.

- **Returning to your physical state of consciousness unintentionally.**

This is often caused by random thoughts directed toward your physical body. You must focus and maintain your full attention on the nonphysical environment and energy body that you are experiencing. Never think about your physical body during inner explorations.

- **Poor perception or your awareness is unclear or dreamlike.**

Firmly demand clarity until your perception is clear. Commands such as "Clarity now!" or "Awareness now!" will sharpen your awareness. Focus on a specific item or area in the immediate environment that you are exploring.

- **A panic attack or any feeling of fear or anxiety.**

Surround yourself with an impenetrable wall or globe of protective white light. If needed repeat to yourself that you are safe and secure. Refer to <u>The Secret of the Soul</u> pages 211-239 for additional information. Fear-based thoughts can and will create fearful form-based results. Sending love to any fear can also be effective.

- **Experiencing your body as formless conscious energy. This may be accompanied by 360-degree perception.**

This is the normal recognition of our inner self beyond the astral dimension. We are formless (pure consciousness) currently using a human form for experience. Our natural perception is 360 degrees. This is a positive indication that you have progressed spiritually.

- **An extremely loud noise experienced during altered or trance states.**

This can be startling and is likely the result of a sudden energy opening and surge emanating from the chakra located in your forehead (third eye). It's a positive indication of an opening or shift in your energy field.

- **The experience of seeing through your closed physical eyelids during meditation, sleep, or any altered state.**

A common occurrence, this is a positive indication that you are experiencing a shift of consciousness. This occurs when your awareness is transferred to your less dense energy body (etheric) but you remain partially attached to your physical body. To initiate an OBE, direct your focus to a location away from your body. An effective command is "Door Now!"

- **Entering the vibrational state but being unable to expand or enhance your state of consciousness beyond your physical limits.**

This is a frequently reported event. Allow the vibrations to expand through you, then mentally direct and focus your complete attention away from your physical body and toward another area of your home. Direct your awareness with a power statement such as "Door now!" Focusing on rolling sideways is another effective way to disengage from the physical. "Roll now." Refer to Adventures beyond the Body pages 164-168 for more detailed information.

- **Entering a nonphysical environment containing cloud-like forms. They may appear as holographic images with varying degrees of density.**

You are observing nonphysical thought-energy forms, the direct result of focused thought on a nonphysical energy environment. Thought shapes energy in every dimensional reality.

- **Your immediate surroundings appear to be a near duplicate of your physical environment with minor changes, such as colors, furniture shape, or location.**

You are currently experiencing your slowest frequency energy body and observing the parallel energy dimension closest in density to the physical universe. As you move inward this environment will dissolve and a new reality will be experienced.

- **The vivid sensation of external thoughts, images, or pictures entering your mind during an altered state.**

This is the natural form of nonphysical communication. Remain calm as you allow the images to unfold. During these experiences, the universal method of communication is achieved by direct thought and image transference. Be aware that this may also be a form of inner communication with a higher aspect of your inner self.

- **Becoming disoriented during altered states.**

Remain calm and cease all forward or inner motion.

Center your state of consciousness through firm affirmations. Silently demand and repeat one of the following phrases: "Awareness now!", "Clarity now!", "Focus now!" or "Stability now!" If possible select a single item or image in your immediate nonphysical environment and focus on it. Never think about or focus on any aspect of your physical body.

- **The perception of motion through any kind of entrance: doors, portals, tunnels, cave entrances, windows, and openings of all shapes and sizes.**

Entranceways, doors, and caves often represent the beginning or entrance into a different energy/vibrational environment. When entering a new reality, remember to stabilize your energy body and focus only on that reality. Repeat a firm affirmation such as, "Stability now!"

Note that this is often our mind's interpretation of an inner shift of consciousness, or a potential transit point or opening in the energy field dividing two different frequency levels (non-physical energy environments, realities, or dimensions.) This perception is heavily is influenced by our beliefs.

- **Observing or confronting a strange or frightening form, creature, or being of any kind. This may also manifest as a personal challenge, obstacle, or test.**

Generally, this is an energy projection of our own inner fear-based thoughts and emotions. It is a consciously created opportunity for us to confront and resolve our personal fears, blocks or limitations. The most effective way to eliminate a problem or fear is to face it. Sending love to fear is one of the best ways to dissipate this energy. This is a highly effective opportunity to confront and resolve our inner fears and blocks. This process of confrontational learning experiences is often referred to as spiritual initiations. Refer to page 250, <u>Adventures beyond the Body</u>, and page 213 <u>The Secret of the Soul</u>.

- **Rapidly changing or shifting scenes or environments.**

This is often a lack of concentration on your part. Your state of consciousness is fluctuating. Focus and lock your awareness on a single object in your immediate environment and this will cease. This may also be an indication that you are in a non-consensus reality. "Focus now" is an effective response.

- **A distortion or reversal of perception.**

As consciousness, we do not possess biological eyes or ears. Your mind has molded an energy body and perceptions that conform to your physical-like self-conception. We are not human animals; our natural nonphysical perception is 360 degrees. Through experience we learn to adapt to our natural and expanded observation capabilities.

- **Losing conscious control in the middle of an altered state or exploration of consciousness.**

Mentally demand your full awareness to be immediately present, "Awareness now! Focus Now!" Any random thoughts focused on your physical body will immediately return you to your physical state of consciousness.

- **The sudden or gradual feeling of heaviness, lack of mobility or vision during any exploration of consciousness.**

An inadequate percentage of your conscious awareness is concentrated within your currently activated energy body. Firmly demand an increase in your focus with an affirmation, "Awareness or focus now!" This will increase the amount of conscious awareness within your energy body. We must learn how to effectively focus our awareness to become an effective explorer of consciousness.

- **The perception of becoming tangled or restricted by any nonphysical item, structure, or environment.**

Remain calm and simply direct yourself away from the obstacle. This issue often represents a self-created energy block or limit that requires resolution. Demand an immediate shift or enhancement in your state of consciousness. Silently repeating "Next level now!" or "Awareness now!" can be effective.

- **Your immediate surroundings appear to rapidly melt or dissolve around you.**

You are energetically shifting or moving your awareness inwardly within your multidimensional self. Focus completely on your new environment. All external changes of your surroundings reflect the internal shifts of your consciousness. You are always the creative center of your experiences. What you perceive is in vibrational alignment with your current energy body. Your reality is always relative to your personal density. It is helpful to immediately stabilize your state of consciousness when moving into a different vibrational environment.

- **Entering a complete void or empty space.**

You have entered a formless area that exists within all nonphysical dimensions. This is an uninhabited nonphysical area that is currently unaffected by collective or individual thought projections. Voids can be very responsive to our focused thought. Remain calm and silently demand, "Higher self now or Next Level Now!"

- **Cobwebs, lightness, or heaviness in any part of the body, a sinking or falling sensation.**

This is a common experience that occurs when entering an altered state of consciousness or trance state. Continue to focus on your intention for exploration.

- **Experiencing an elevator, ramps, steps, or staircase of any kind. Any perception and manifestation of levels or movement between levels.**

This is a common perception during inner explorations; our mind's form-based interpretation of a shift in our state of consciousness. It can also indicate the inner motion between energy sub-levels of a given dimensional reality within you. As an example — consider climbing steps as a path to a higher (lighter) vibrational environment. Stabilize after every major change or enhancement with a firm command. "Focus now!"

- **The sensation of spontaneous movement to a new reality. This is often intense. Sometimes referred to as astral wind.**

Your higher mind/self is directing your experience. Allow the experience to develop. Your awareness is being moved to a different energy location, often to provide a learning opportunity (simulation) for your personal development. Demand "Awareness now" to stabilize yourself after any shift of consciousness.

- **Spontaneously experiencing or being drawn into a different time line.**

You may be experiencing a present or 'past' experience and a life-learning situation. Often this is a lesson orchestrated by your higher self. Observe the energy display carefully for this may relate to an issue, relationship, or block in your current life. We are often drawn to unresolved energies that manifest as nonphysical experiences and lessons (simulations).This is a positive and powerful opportunity to confront and resolve long-standing energy issues or blocks.

- **Being locked within a single reality. How do I move from one dimension to another?**

You must learn to develop your multidimensional skills and your ability to shift your consciousness beyond your current energy body. During an altered state the focused command, "Next level now!" can be an effective approach. This process of inner exploration is explained in all of my books.

- **Experiencing any manifestation of the vibrational state including unusual sounds, vibrations, voices, or energy sensations as you sleep. This includes catalepsy and perceiving through closed eyes. Refer to page 157 in <u>Adventures beyond the Body.</u>**

Remain calm, all are positive indications that you are in an altered state of consciousness. This also suggests that you are out-of-sync with your physical body. Surrender to the vibrational sensations, and allow the energy to expand throughout your entire being. To initiate an OBE, direct your full attention to a location away from your physical body. "Door now!" is one example. A focused and repeated thought command in the present tense will create the best results. Make all commands forceful and expect immediate results.

- **The sensation of sinking, spinning, flying, floating, or any perception of motion.**

Stay centered while having this positive experience. Your nonphysical energy body is activated and in motion. Any sensation of inner motion may indicate you are in the process of shifting your state of consciousness inward and within your multidimensional self. This may also indicate movement beyond the physical body. Surrender and flow with the motion allowing it to expand. To initiate a spiritual experience, silently demand "Higher self now!"

- **Experiences involving the perception of cleansing or adjustment; this may include bathing in water, fire, rebirth etc.**

Any form of cleansing is our mind's interpretation of a vibrational adjustment or the potential removal of negative emotional patterns or blocks from your nonphysical body. This is often an enhancement or realignment in our state of consciousness and energy body. As this is a positive energy event, relax and enjoy the entire process.

- **The sensation of rapid movement through multiple layers of color, energy, haze, or rings. This can be intense and disorienting.**

Your conscious awareness is moving/shifting inward within your multidimensional self. This is classic inter-dimensional exploration; an essential skill to develop. "Stability or focus now" can help to stabilize your state during and after all shifts of consciousness. Immediately after the motion begins demand "Higher self now!" This can help to initiate a profound spiritual experience.

- **Flying or falling in an altered state or dream.**

This is often your mind's interpretation of a shift or transition of consciousness or an OBE. Immediately demand and repeat, "Awareness now" to become more aware during your experience. For more detailed information on dream awakening and conversion refer to <u>Adventures beyond the Body</u>, pages 181-191.

- **Experiencing a state of confusion or disorientation.**

Mentally demand the focus and stability of awareness you require during your experience. Make it a focused demand in the present tense: "Clarity now! Stability now! Awareness now! Focus now!"

- **During your exploration your new environment becomes different than your current physical reality.**

This is a normal experience. Your consciousness has entered a different energy dimension and reality. The further inward you explore, the less dense and more thought responsive is the experienced energy environment. It is a clear indication that you have shifted your awareness inward to another dimensional reality.

- **Your nonphysical body, arms, or legs begin to dissolve. This can occur quickly when you stare at (confront) your nonphysical hands.**

Soul/consciousness is not a form-based being. As we prolong our presence in a nonphysical state there is a tendency to revert to our natural (formless) state of consciousness. As we prolong our nonphysical state of awareness, we will begin to experience aspects of our inner multidimensional self.

- **Dual consciousness. Your awareness is partially in your physical body and also in your nonphysical energy body or in two different nonphysical bodies simultaneously.**

Since consciousness is not physical in nature, it has the innate ability to experience multiple realities at the same time. An aspect of our consciousness currently exists in all dimensions and has the ability to move inwardly within the nonphysical interior of the universe. To eliminate dual consciousness, focus on a single environment or object and demand "Awareness now!"

- **Becoming blocked or restricted by a wall, floor, ceiling or a perceived structure of any kind.**

Generally, barriers are a manifestation of our own self-created limits. It can represent a possible limitation that we have accepted or created ourselves. This presents a valuable opportunity to confront a personal energy block and resolve it. It may also be the border to a private consensus reality created by group collective consciousness.

During your altered state, focus and demand the answer or resolution to any issue or obstacle that you encounter. We must confront, resolve, and release all recurring energy issues or they will continue to manifest in both our physical and nonphysical lives. Enhance your state by silently repeating a focused command such as "Awareness now! Next level now! Higher self now!"

If needed, confront the barrier or block with a focused challenge, "What do you represent?" During an altered state, projecting love to a recurring energy issue is one method to resolve it. Refer to page 233-234, The Secret of the Soul.

Review of Key Points in Part One

- We are a non-physical, immortal and highly creative species.
- All form-based reality in every dimension is crystalized thought.
- We possess the ability to shape and mold our reality with our focused thoughts.
- Our natural environment is nonphysical and extremely thought responsive.
- The complete universe - seen and unseen - is a multidimensional continuum.
- We are multidimensional beings currently extending our awareness into a temporary biological vehicle of expression.
- We are a species that learns and evolves by direct experience in many dimensional realities. We become that which we wish to learn.
- All of our current concepts of linear time, manmade beliefs and biological life and death have no reference to an immortal nonphysical species.
- It is essential for us to learn how to completely control our powerful creative ability in order to successfully coexist in an instant thought responsive environment.
- The physical universe acts as a slowed down training and educational reality for developing consciousness/soul. We learn from direct intense experiences.
- We create our own personalized educational curriculum by the life choices and actions we make. Each soul learns

and evolves at their own pace, for they create their own educational lessons and dramas.

- The dense training realities of the physical and astral dimensions provide a highly effective method to cloister the young, immature and developing souls within a dense series of training environments. As they spiritually evolve they become energetically able to enter and coexist with the higher dimensional realities.

- The countless life forms and environments of the physical and astral dimensions provide an endless spectrum of training vehicles and opportunities for training developing consciousness.

- Through multiple experiences (lives) we eventually evolve from the intense training ground of matter and form.

- We graduate from the dense training realities when we exhibit complete responsibility and control of our thought projections and express the qualities of a highly evolved spiritual being (love, fearlessness, self-sacrifice, etc.).

- We graduate when we become fully conscious multidimensional beings.

We are immortal, powerful beings that create our reality now and continue to do so when we exit our body. It is essential that we learn and practice methods to enhance and expand our state of consciousness beyond the limits of the physical. During all explorations of consciousness focus on experiencing your spiritual essence or higher self. Make this your primary goal in this life. Becoming an active explorer of consciousness is the key to our awakening and liberation.

Only when are we are evolved and spiritually mature are we ready to dwell within the magnificent instant thought responsive realities of our true nonphysical home. This inward journey of consciousness within us is the direct evolutionary path of consciousness/soul.

Closing Thoughts

"Remember the entrance to the sanctuary is inside you."

Rumi

A bold vision of life and death is now spreading throughout the world. Profound experiences are not reserved for just a few special or gifted people; instead it our universal birthright and our destiny as soul. It is our great task to open our minds and hearts to our full potential. This requires a reappraisal of our long-held theories, beliefs and practices, allowing us to spiritually grow.

We have learned that the transition of consciousness at death can be an event shrouded in fear or a powerful launch pad for profound awakening and transformation. We and we alone determine our focused spiritual intention and the trajectory we travel in life and in death. By becoming proactive and creating a personal spiritual action plan now, we can achieve our ultimate goals.

We can also physically, mentally, and emotionally assist another who is ending this earthly experience by providing an environment of serenity and love, creating the conditions that encourage a transformation at the highest level. Our evolution is just beginning; let us be prepared and take action.

PART TWO

Approaching Death With Wisdom and Grace

Approaching Death with Wisdom and Grace

Spending hours, weeks and sometimes even months with the families and friends of those who have been given a terminal diagnosis, I found myself journaling to offset some difficult emotions. An unintended outcome of this note taking was a clear picture of what worked and didn't work when it came to the spiritual and emotional well-being of the dying.

To that end, the content of Part Two is focused on three elements:

- Bringing comfort to the physical and emotional body.
- Gently encouraging the soul to journey to the higher self.
- Releasing the spirit from ties to the physical world.

Sharing my real life doula experiences from homes, hospice houses and residential living facilities is intended to provide you with information you can use for transition planning.

As much as we'd like to avoid facing it, physical death will come to all of us. We could die gradually from a disease or natural aging. Perhaps there will be a sudden death, such as a tragic accident or an unexpected medical event. But it will happen to us and to everyone we know.

Due to advancements in medical technology, many of us will have the opportunity at some point to be a part of someone's gradual death. Maybe we will have time to discuss and organize the intellectual, spiritual, and emotional desires of our parent, sibling or long-time friend. But what if there is a sudden transition where there is little or no time for developing a plan? It is not too late to have a profound impact on any soul that is crossing. The techniques and strategies to assist someone in reaching their higher self can work regardless of when and where they have passed.

I have included the prayers, meditations, and ceremony scripts that I have written and put into practice with those who were in their final hours. Feel free to use them in your own situation and customize the words to meet the needs of your family. All deaths are different, so use this information to supplement your personal situation while acting in accordance with the wishes of the dying.

Spiritual evolution is possible before, during and even after the physical death. However, this is easier to accomplish when you have knowledge of the dying process and feel more comfortable with what to expect. Whether there is a terminal illness or sudden death, having a spiritual support plan already in place will help you to navigate through a highly emotional time.

Susan

Please Note: The names and health specifics used in this book have been changed to protect the privacy of the patients and their families. Do not substitute this information for professional medical or legal advice.

CHAPTER 1

———— ✦ ————

Prepare for a Spiritual Transition

*"Since the afterlife is thought-responsive, our last domi-
nant emotions and thoughts at the time of transition
can influence and mold the subtle energy environments
we experience after death."*

WILLIAM BUHLMAN

YOUR LIFE CAN change in a matter of minutes. If there is something that you want to do, a conversation that you need to begin, or a place that you would like to see—do it. One doctor's
appointment, one afternoon behind the wheel of a car, or one
step in the wrong direction can change your life forever.

When we are young and healthy, it's easy to believe that when
we die we will go to some heavenly paradise where we will all live
happily ever after. However, when we are sick or injured, looking
death in the eye, it can be very frightening to face an unknown
as vast as the afterlife. I learned about this one morning as I had
a silent visit with a sweet lady who had only days to live.

Miss Bess ate her breakfast slowly, thoughtfully. Seated on
the side of the bed she was a little unsteady, so the hospice
medical staff thought it would be wise to have someone with

her. As the volunteer on duty, I would be her guardian while she ate. Occasionally she would glance my way and raise her painted-on eyebrows with just a hint of sparkle left in her eyes. She was wearing her own matching nightgown and robe, with her hair pulled back into a neat twist and bright red color on her lips. Focused on the cinnamon bun in front of her, she didn't speak—she just stared out the window at nothing in particular. Bite after deliberate bite, I could almost read her mind. "How did I get to this point in my life? Why is my body failing me? What happens next?"

Bill and I had just celebrated our twin sons' thirtieth birthday. We all met for lunch in Leesburg at a microbrewery cafe the day before. As I looked at my two grown men across the table, I remember thinking how fast time had flown by. Had it really been thirty years since they were babies? So when I looked at Miss Bess—who was probably about thirty years older than I am—it hit home. In another flash of time, that will be me. What will I be thinking, sitting on the side of the bed struggling with the simplest of tasks? Will I be afraid, thinking, "What happens next? Where will I go when my body dies?" Or will I say "I have completed this life as I had planned. Now, I'm ready for my next adventure!"

When we returned home, Bill and I talked about it. After a lengthy discussion, it occurred to us both that at this point in our life we still have the opportunity to assert a great deal of input regarding our own transitions, from both a physical and a spiritual perspective. We can create a natural environment that supports the elevation to our higher self at the time when the physical body stops functioning; but more importantly, we can work on our readiness today.

Getting Started

People do not want to talk about death in general, much less their own, but this failure to communicate about the most guaranteed event in human life can lead to misunderstanding and regret. Families are unsure what the dying person wants, so they layer their own principles onto the situation. People often fail to say simple but meaningful things before someone dies and are filled with remorse for years. A spouse or partner may have some thoughts about their mate's wishes, but bow to a traditional service suggested by a funeral director—because that's the way it's done. There is little time to think, much less plan a meaningful transition or ceremony.

Greg had been diagnosed in mid-July and at the end of August it was determined that hospice was appropriate. He had esophageal cancer that had spread quickly. Understandably, his wife was very upset, gently wiping at her constant tears. I spent some time talking to her about his life growing up and their life together as a couple. They had been married for thirty-two years, but this past year was undoubtedly the best year of their lives. With all four parents gone, they were finally able to do some of the things they had planned. She spoke of the traveling they had considered, some of the new adventures they would try, and the places they would see that had been on their 'bucket list.' None of those things would happen now. We talked about what she would do after he was gone, but to her the future looked bleak. I gave them both a Reiki experience on Sunday morning. I felt a message from him that he was worried about her. It was so strong that I unexpectedly responded out loud, "She's going to be OK." During our session I noticed that his hands and arms seemed to relax and slide down from the tense position he was holding over his torso. There was so much energy in the room that the hairs on my arm stood up. I believe that he had many unseen visitors lining up to help him. I went back on Monday to see if I could offer any more comfort but he had died early that morning.

This is just one of many examples illustrating why we need to start work on our end-of-life plan today. Serious illness and death can come so quickly. There you are making plans for your future and in the blink of an eye the future is reduced to just weeks. If you are reading this book, then you already have begun the process.

So how do we get started? First, it is important to understand that impending death is more than a medical situation. Along with the physical impact to our body, there are social, spiritual, and emotional implications. Often we are more wrapped up in the health and family issues than in the spiritual objective, and because of that we lose a beautiful chance to advance our soul beyond the primary astral levels. If we become more comfortable with the conditions surrounding the physical event, then we can better direct our focus to the ultimate spiritual experience.

Issues that can slow our Spiritual Freedom

When you or a loved one receives a terminal diagnosis, what feels like a thousand changes will happen all at once, and often most of these are not supportive of our fundamental goals. We are having a human experience after all, so we can expect many different demands tug at us, redirecting our mind toward resolving material issues instead of focusing on our core intention. The influences that are swirling around us should be recognized and resolved as much as possible to allow us to focus on our spiritual goals. Being aware of what will potentially happen to us or our loved one is the first step to moving beyond the physical issues and focusing on the actions that support an enlightened transition at the time of death.

Physical Changes

During a long illness, our body transforms and we don't know what to expect from day to day. Discomfort can be successfully managed through pharmaceuticals and complimentary therapies such as massage, Reiki, and guided visualizations. Even so, a person may not be used to feeling bad and can be consumed with the medication schedule instead of their upcoming ethereal journey. Even the very anticipation of physical pain can lead to anxiety that can sap one's strength. The resulting weakness can make one feel like they have lost their sense of self. An overall feeling of helplessness can make spiritual preparation a low priority.

The more we become informed about what to expect in the body, the better we can adjust when those changes occur. With the physical issues addressed, we can be more present for spiritual progress.

Relationships with Friends and Family

Your community activity as well as your family relationships may change. There may be financial issues related to medical care or family members who are verbalizing conflict about the remaining estate. Companionship is more difficult as friends find it uncomfortable to maintain a relationship with those who can no longer function as they have in the past.

"I'm not ready to die. This is too sudden." If there is unfinished business, communication to resolve it can be hindered. Missed events might be a frustration as the dying person may have wanted to stay around to meet their first grandchild but now feels that this may not be possible.

Everything that was familiar and comfortable is about to be replaced by a totally new and unknown environment. It can drive awkward situations if we do not know how to support a changed relationship. As friends and family members, the more we know as we enter this phase the more helpful we can be. This allows us to keep focused on the truly essential part of our spiritual evolution.

Environmental Modifications can be Unsettling

Think about the basics that you control every day that you are alive—what you wear, what you eat, and even how your bedroom is arranged. And then consider what it would feel like to be totally dependent on others to make these selections for you. First, where are you located? Are you upstairs in a back bedroom or down in the main living area? What is the room temperature? Are you cold while others are enjoying the breeze coming through the open window? What is the bed position? Are you artificially propped up and not comfortable? Maybe you would rather be sitting in a chair. Is there a bright light overhead that you wish could be dimmed? What about the noise level? Are you longing for soft music, while all you can hear is the washing machine because you are located next to the laundry area?

While in an in-patient facility, I was sitting with a gentleman who was sleeping soundly and I wondered how much of the activity around him he could hear. The vacuum was running up and down the hallway for at least 20 minutes. A receptionist was answering the phone every few minutes with the same greeting: "Hello, this is Nancy. How may I direct your call? One moment, please." Some nurses were laughing over an inside joke and the restroom door across the hall was opened and closed several times. Based on my experience, this was an unusual occurrence—a perfect storm of noisy activity. But noise is important to consider as you think about your resting area. I went over and closed his door to block out most of the fray.

Later in this book, there are some helpful hints about creating a sacred space and how you can communicate your desires to your caretakers.

Emotional Turmoil may be Evident or Hidden behind a Stoic Personality

Many people are afraid of death because of a strict religious upbringing. Others are afraid of leaving loved ones alone. Maybe it is as simple as fear of the unknown. I've seen melancholy, remorse, and impatience in the dying. Some may feel bad about abandoning people who count on them financially or socially. They might be worried about making other people sad, so they try to appear content in order to keep from upsetting others. If there are ongoing disputes where amends have not been made, it can cause anxiety.

The family members around the sick person may begin to experience grief before the death even occurs. This can manifest as anger, depression, and frustration that interfere with spiritual support. Withdrawal and avoidance may seem like a personal affront, but it's just a human way of handling an unwanted situation. To be fair, I have also seen relief (from a distressing illness) and contentment (from a life well lived.) The mix of emotions can change several times during the day.

I spent some time every week sharing Reiki with a woman in her eighties named Elsie. She had beautiful skin and snow-white hair that was combed back away from her crystal-blue eyes. During one of our sessions, she began to cry. I inquired if she was afraid. She replied by shaking her head back and forth with her hands covering her eyes. "Well. Are you sad?" I asked her. "No. I am very happy," she responded in her heavy Germanic accent. "I talked to God today and he told me, Elsie, it's gonna be OK."

If you were to take your last breath tomorrow, would you have any regret? Is there an event you feel guilty about? How about unresolved anger toward someone you know or have had business with in the past? Any of these emotional issues can slow down your spiritual transition. Can you resolve any of these today?

A woman I know had a difficult relationship with her stepdaughter, Lulu, which climaxed in a full-blown event during a family outing. Many regrettable things were said and Wanda told me that she would never get over the insults that were sent her way. Due to her illness, time was short to resolve this conflict so I politely mentioned to another family member that there would be regrets if there was no attempt at reconciliation. "This is not a good way to leave things as she draws closer to the end." Lulu provided some weak (interpreted as insincere) attempts at an explanation, but her apology went without acceptance. When Wanda passed, the conflict was still as fresh in her mind as it was on the day of the argument. Wanda and her stepdaughter will likely both continue to sustain this dispute even after her transition and they may again face this tumultuous connection in another life.

In this book are examples and techniques that can be used today to eliminate some of the unfinished business we might face in our last days. This can reduce the impact of emotional disturbance during our dying hours, bringing our heart back to an ideal spiritual transition.

Spiritual Knowledge versus Religious Training

How many of us feel that the religious teachings we were given as a child are no longer relevant to the knowledge we have since accumulated? Sometimes people will revert to their traditional ideologies due to fear or peer pressure. Often family members assume that you want to follow your early religious training or feel that it is better to be safe than sorry. Maybe they cannot ask you because of your current medical condition, so they make assumptions.

When death becomes imminent, many people tend to grasp traditional religious symbolism. Voices become hushed, heads are bowed, and church hymns hit the CD players. Almost all Christian patients have statues, crosses, and scripture cards in their room, even though they haven't been to church in years. This can be an artificial insurance policy. "If I put all this around them, then God will know that they belong in heaven. Maybe the lack of recent dedication will be overlooked." This could be a move to avoid any perceived punishment in the afterlife. Would this still be in line with your way of thinking? Readiness to move on is different for everyone. How ready will you be? Does your family really know what you consider important or are you counting on them to make choices for you?

Overall vulnerability due to loss of control can affect our spiritual progress. How much of this can you clarify now so that you have fewer issues when death occurs?

Leaving it for Someone Else to do

You might ask why we should plan for our own physical surroundings during the time of our death. Why can't we just let someone else handle the details as we take our last few breaths? Isn't that what the doctors are for? Aren't there standard protocols that I will have to follow as I spend my last days or weeks under the care of whatever my insurance plan will cover? If I plan for my own death, will I bring it on prematurely? Perhaps you think that professionals in the undertaking business can provide your family with good advice. Possibly, but I don't want to leave my transition to chance, hoping someone will know my desires and provide exactly what I need.

During the final stages of our physical life, our instinct for survival can be stronger than the quest for spiritual awareness. Drugs and surgical solutions that have not been tested on the elderly are implemented to keep the heart beating long after the pleasure of life has diminished, sometimes creating more health problems than before. People become so desperate to stay in this physical world for even a few more weeks or months that they are willing to sacrifice quality of life for quantity of days. When faced with a diagnosis of a life-limiting illness, people tend to turn over control of their medical care to those who are experts and perhaps their spiritual care along with it.

We have power even in the end of this life and should do whatever we can to exercise it. You can document what you would like to have as your last physical environment, right down to the music and lighting. It is essential to seize the moment and be the masters of our destiny. We are here on Earth as part of our soul's education. What better way to use these learnings than in our own transition to the next level? As most of us do not know how and when we will die, being prepared should be a top priority on our to-do list.

CHAPTER 2

⚬

Create a Safe Harbor— Bringing Comfort to Others

"With life as short as a half taken breath, don't plant anything but love."

RUMI

To KEEP HER from being hurt, Sam made me promise not to tell his wife this story. (She already knew, he just didn't remember.) He had gone to the doctor and was told that there was nothing more that could be done for him. He should just go home and make himself as comfortable as possible because he was going to die. Sam slapped his thigh with anger as he relayed this news to me. He couldn't believe that the doctor had given up on him. He refused to accept the prognosis. He believes (pretends?) that his wife doesn't know and the two of them live day to day much like they had before that fateful day at the doctor's office. Rather than use the precious time that they have together to address any unresolved issues in their relationship and plan for a spiritual transition, they continue to arrange their days around TV shows, events at the Senior Center, and a few unwelcome family gatherings.

When a person is dying, the body has already set itself on an irreversible path. It knows what to do, and the physical changes resulting from the experience will happen on schedule. The emotional and spiritual release is more pliable. This is where we can make a difference. The following information is designed not to ease your grief or satisfy the desires of the family, but to help you focus on the person who is leaving their physical body. It is for their successful transition to the nonphysical world.

Entering the Space

Sometimes it helps to stop for just a moment before you enter the room. Take a few deep breaths and bring yourself into the present moment. Clear the activities of the day from your mind and direct your thoughts to your friend in the next room. Do your best to leave your tensions and stress at the door. Enter the room with a relaxed but caring attitude. It is OK to shed a few tears during your visit, but if you feel a fit of hysteria coming on, you should probably excuse yourself until you can pull it together.

Your body language can say more than you think. This is the time to be comforting and supportive. Approaching someone with folded arms or clenched hands can send a different message than your words do. Be conscious about making kind eye contact, offering genuine smiles, using caring touch, and giving gentle hugs.

How to Begin the Discussion

As illustrated above in Sam's story, many people are afraid to talk about serious illness, let alone impending death. But to reduce the chance that you will have regrets after the transition, you really need to scale those walls of fear. In the beginning, most people would like to have a normal conversation that doesn't revolve around their prognosis. During the final stages of their illness, a more intimate talk may be desired.

Many people who are at the end of their life have knowledge of their upcoming departure. If you listen closely, you will probably hear your loved one hint about their condition or even test what you know. "I'm not getting around like I used to. I guess my time is about up." Or you might hear "I don't think I'll make it to your Thanksgiving dinner this year." Let your loved one take the lead on the discussion. You might be asked a question directly. "Do you think I am going to die soon?" You could respond with a question. "Why would you say/ask that?" or "How are you feeling about your condition?" At this point, your opinion might not be what they are looking for. Your friend could be throwing out a hint that they need to tell you what is on their mind.

I sat with a lady named Hattie for a few hours. She was several weeks away from her transition and still communicating rather well. We talked about a few harmless topics like flowers, TV shows, and the meals in the facility. She turned to me with a very serious look and said, "Are you here waiting for me to die?" I replied, "No, I'm just visiting. Why do you ask? Do you think you are going to die?" She thought for a moment and answered, "To tell you the truth, I just don't know what to think these days." If I had been a family member or close friend I would have pursued this further, giving her an opportunity to talk about any fears she might have or unfinished business that I could help with.

The Basics

From prognosis to actively dying, there will be a range of talking points. This can span from "How's the weather?" to "Before I go, I'd like to tell you how much I love you." So as you review the options listed below, be sensitive to the point in time and follow the direction to where your loved one guides you. If you are not sure you are saying the right thing, ask yourself these three questions:

Am I being authentic?
Am I being calm?
Am I being caring?

Don't feel pressured to answer a detailed medical question. If you feel unqualified to provide a response, it's OK to say "I don't know." This is not the time to conduct some online research and pass on your findings to someone who is suffering from a terminal illness. If there is a disease or condition-based answer you must know, please consult the doctors, nurses, or social workers who have been assigned to your case.

Don't provide false hope. "Hang in there. I think you can beat this thing!" If someone is terminal, you are only fueling an internal conflict of 'Should I fight to stay or prepare to release?' This may involve your acceptance of the inevitable as well. There will come a point where you will have to stop trying to have your loved one undergo every possible treatment and/or procedure that has been associated with the disease. "How would you feel about taking a break from all these procedures for a little while?" Respect the decision of the patient regarding when to stop.

Do be aware of your timing. There is no need to get very specific about how long someone has to live or what physical issues they can expect. After all, each death is different. "What is the most important thing I can do for you?" "Tell me exactly what I can do to put your mind at ease."

Dwayne had come into our hospice facility earlier in the week. He was younger than most of the others in the house. He wasn't wearing the standard pajama or hospital gown, so his St. Lucia T-shirt prompted our discussion of his love for the Caribbean. He had traveled there every year on his birthday, often inviting perfect strangers from the airplane to attend his celebration. He felt like it was a place where he could be himself, with no one asking anything of him. I could tell there was more to this story, but I didn't want to dig too deep. He would tell me if he wanted me to know. I shared Reiki with him a few times. I was pleased when he said he could feel the energy transfer. He noticed when my hands became very warm. Because he was unfamiliar with Reiki, I found those words very reassuring—hey it's working! During one session he had a phone call from a family member who was cleaning out his apartment. I heard him tell her that he didn't know what to do with this item or that. Trying not to be obviously listening, I could see he was getting upset as he used the terms 'take it to the dump' and 'I don't know, do whatever you want with it.' When he hung up, there were tears in his eyes. He looked at me and said "They're taking my stuff. They're getting rid of everything." I felt his pain. He apologized for the tears. I tried to comfort him with "Those are only things—physical objects. What's really important are the relationships you've nurtured, the memories you've created. No one can take away the experiences you've had." After thinking about it later, I realized that it wasn't necessarily the 'stuff' he was concerned about. By closing the lease on his apartment and disposing of all of his personal possessions, it became very real. He wasn't going home from here. It brought the idea of death one step closer and he was afraid. So if you are ever in a relationship with a dying person, try not to talk about packing up (disposing of) their physical life unless they take the lead. They may not be ready.

Listen. I mean really listen. People have such valuable insights into life when it is nearing an end for them. Ask open-ended questions about how they are feeling. Offer your assistance to help with those things that are now too difficult for them. "What do I need to know to help you get through this time in your life?" Asking questions about their life's work, their family, their hobbies, and interests may help you to establish the necessary actions to tie up any loose ends. This is the time for life reviews and sharing memories.

Do not compare symptoms. "I had a pain just like that. My doctor told me that if I took a walk every day, it would help. Have you tried walking?" "My neighbor's husband died from that. He only lived for three months after they diagnosed him. You're lucky that you've already made it for four months." More appropriately is "How are you feeling? Can I get anything to make you more comfortable?"

This is also not the time to pull a confession from someone. "I just need to know. What did you say to Aunt Betty that made her cry at cousin Bobo's wedding?" Allow the person to lead the conversation in the direction that they need. "Do you need me to contact anyone? Are there any messages that I can give for you?"

Don't overthink your choice of topic. Many people don't know what to say, so they totally avoid a visit that would force them into a conversation. You have known this person for some time so choose a topic that he would have enjoyed before the diagnosis, even politics if that has always been a lively subject for discussion. Start by asking a question. "I heard that George Clooney was going to run for President. What do you think his chances are?" "Did you hear that Congress was going to repeal the bicycle tax? Do you think they should?" You will know right away if this line of conversation isn't welcome. Until they begin to withdrawal, most people want to maintain some kind of normalcy in their lives. Another idea is to explore a hobby or interest. "I know you are interested in dinosaur bones, so I brought this article from the <u>New York Times</u> that talks about some new discoveries in Utah."

Be aware of your tone. I hear people using 'baby talk' with the dying. It makes me cringe. Use your grown-up voice. Don't use pet names unless they were relevant prior to this stage in their life. For example, if you always called her 'Aunt Sissy' while growing up, continue to do so. "How's my little boo-boo doing today?" comes off as condescending. Using a hushed voice to talk about them to others as if they are not in the room is insulting. "Does she want anything to eat?" If she is eating, then she can hear you and respond herself. On the other hand, a loud, overzealous "Hey, Uncle Buck you aren't flirting with all these young pretty nurses are you?" might be out of place. Keep a natural tone and conversation style. If in doubt, think about how you would like to be approached under the same circumstances.

Be very careful about assuming religious beliefs and needs. If they did not embrace Christianity (or any other formal religion) during their life, then it is not likely that it is appropriate for them now. It would be cruel to tell someone that they will go to hell if they don't have a priest give them the last sacrament. And this is even worse if it was done after they could not speak for themselves. As one is dying, they become busy evaluating their life's purpose. They may already be fairly critical of themselves. Do not try to pass your attitudes onto them. At the same time, if someone wants to have their rosary beads laced around their hands (even if you don't believe that it is helpful) then make it so. You can still provide positive affirmations and guidance for them to consciously become their higher self.

It was the first of August when I met Daniel. He was in his young fifties with early-onset dementia. He was not communicating, but was restless, so I sat with him while we listened to music. He seemed to calm down as I added some soothing affirmations. He began to sleep, but I didn't want to leave him alone just yet. I walked around his room and picked up a photo album that I thought I could use for conversation later. The cover read "Danny's Baptism, May 20XX." I thought how nice that he at least had that experience with his namesake grandson. However, as I looked through the pictures, I realized that it was this grown man before me that had recently been baptized in a Catholic ceremony. It occurred to me that his family had arranged this ritual for their own benefit, as clearly at this time he was well into an impaired emotional and intellectual condition. If this had been important to Daniel, surely he would have scheduled this earlier in his life. This was an example of a family member exerting their own belief systems on a person who was unable to make this decision on his own.

Stay in the present. It is easy to get caught up in the number of days/hours that are left. It is one of the most frequent questions that I am asked. "How long do you think she has left?" And many times this is asked in front of the resident. To be clear, I have no formal medical training so I would never answer this question with specifics even if I thought I could. My answer is always the same. "She is on her own schedule and will do what feels right for her." And this is true. I have spoken to people who were coherent, mobile, and even energetic who died within days. There have also been times when, as a doula team, we thought death would come within hours and we sat for more than a week. Each person has their own timetable for when they are ready to take those last few steps.

Use comforting expressions. Some examples are: "I love you." "I care about you." "You are not alone." "I am sorry you are in pain." "What can I do to make you more comfortable?" "You are important to me." "I am here for you." Remember, people are probably not looking for advice at this point. They just want to know that someone is there, someone who cares and will hold their hand (even figuratively) through the process.

Help them to share memories. Some people need some reassurance that their life had some meaning, some significance to others. It may be comforting to share memories and confirm meaningful relationships. "Remember that time you tutored those kids at the library? That was so important to them. I saw how enthusiastic they became when they finished a whole book on their own. I'll bet that really helped them to succeed during their teen years. I never asked before, but how did that make you feel when you created that program?"

160

Reconciliation

One of the most difficult things for us, as humans, is to admit that we are wrong. So it follows that saying "I'm sorry" for something either specific or generic is a very hard thing to do. "I am sorry that I complained so much about your traditions. I understand now why you wanted us all together during the holidays." Follow it up with a thank you and that's even better. "Thank you for teaching us the importance of family gatherings."

If you want to stay away from specifics you could use a more general sentiment. "Let's use this time to forgive each other for any issues that we have had in this life." Maybe you aren't sure if there is an issue, but want to make sure you heal any wounds of the heart before saying goodbye.

Appreciation

Gratitude can sometimes help the dying to close the loop on something that they set out to achieve in their life. "I thank you for showing me how to raise nice respectful children." Or "I appreciate all the sacrifices you made so that I could go to college. I know you gave up many vacations to make that happen." "I am so grateful that you taught me how to play the piano. It has given me such pleasure in life."

If you truly cannot find anything to be thankful for then you could say something like this. "Thank you for being an important part of my life. I appreciate the lessons I have gained from your role in it." Saying "thanks" for being such a great mother—when she really wasn't and you both know it—would not benefit either of you.

Allowing Detachment through Reassurance

Helping others to let go of things that might be holding them back from continuing their journey is a monumental gift. Barb was a thirty-eight-year-old mother with melanoma. She was leaving behind two small children and a large number of family members and friends. The most beautiful gift her family and friends left her was the repeated assurance that her son and daughter would be cared for. They did not want her to be in discomfort any longer, extending her painful life just because she was worried about their future. Once the commitment was made regarding the children, Barb could leave this world and move on with her next adventure. This was a simple act that made a huge difference in her transition.

If you are aware of something that might be keeping your loved one from achieving their ultimate spiritual goal, you could use the following visualization with them. Perhaps you can discuss the possibilities with family and friends so that all known concerns are included. This could be done as a group with each person reciting a single balloon or one person saying it all. This depends on the relationships and things that need to be released. This can be done at any time, whether the person is conscious, actively dying, or recently passed. You know them best.

Balloon Float

(Personalize the examples to the person you are helping.)

Imagine you are standing in the middle of a field. The tall grass gently tickles your ankles and the full sun warms your face. You are alone and content. You are safe, and you know how much you are loved. It is a peaceful day. In your hand is a colorful bouquet of floating balloons. There are many colors, each with a matching ribbon that is firmly in your grasp. A light breeze sends the balloons swaying, creating a rainbow reflection across your skin.

Look up and see the red one. It is big and round and you know it can hold any worries that you have. Put all of your money concerns in that balloon—your taxes, your insurance, your credit cards. Our brother Joshua is taking care of those and everything will be OK. Taxes are filed and your accounts are as they should be. He has all that he needs to make sure everything is handled correctly. So place those cares in that red balloon. All of those money issues are now in the balloon. Take that red ribbon from the group, hold it up, and then let it float into the air. Just let it go. All your concerns about money are now gone.

Now look at the green one. Put your worries about the house in that one. Your family will clean it, fix it, and take care of it. The garden is being tended and the windows have been washed. There is no trouble, because all is taken care of perfectly. The dishes are clean and the houseplants are being watered. All of your concerns about the house are now in that green balloon. Find that green ribbon in the group and pull it out. Let it go; watch the breeze catch it and carry it up to the sky. All of your worries about the house have now floated away.

Look up at the blue one. Your little dog Buffy has been to Aunt Selma's house for the last two weeks and they are getting along fine. So put your worries about Buffy into the blue balloon. She has been fed, bathed, and walked. She is going to be taken care of—spoiled and cuddled just as you want her to be loved. Pick out that blue ribbon from the group, hold it out from the others, and then let it go. Just as the blue balloon floats to the sky, your concerns about Buffy are no longer with you.

Every worry, concern, struggle, fear, or trouble you may have is placed in these balloons and one by one they are released. You are safe and loved. Focus only on the journey ahead and begin to consciously awaken your higher self.

I used this technique on an 85-year-old woman with COPD. She was mobile and communicative. My meeting with her started as a Reiki session, but when her daughter told me that she had trouble sleeping due to so many worries, I changed my tactic to add this visualization to her comfort plan. By the time I had reached the second balloon, Connie had tears in her eyes and was gently sobbing. We ended our session on a positive note with smiles and assurances that all would be well as she began to prepare for her transition.

The Elderly

Many gradual deaths are of elderly persons, those who have lived a long and purposeful life. I am always impressed with the experiences that this generation can pass on to families. But often they feel that they have outlived any purpose and have only become a burden to the world. To ease this worry and assure them that they are appreciated and loved, I developed this verse. This is a prayer that can assist a transition while honoring all that an older person has been through and all that they have given to their family.

We are thankful to have had you in our lives.
Over time, you have taught so many people and have learned just as much in return.
Over time, you have lived through happiness and joyful days.

Over time, you have seen so much and you have come through difficult times with triumph.
Your life has been a gift to us all.
Now is the time to forgive those who have given you challenges.
Now is the time to accept forgiveness from those who have challenged you.
Now is the time to say goodbye, with a heartfelt thank you from all you have served in this life.
We wish for you to have a peaceful journey as you transition to your higher self.

Consider all the changes that an older person has seen in their life. By the very nature of the decades in linear time, they have most likely had more relationships and experiences; they have seen and lived through world wars, economic disasters, and social unrest. They may have watched while many close friends and siblings lived through their last days of life. A number of people tell me that they are the last one of their contemporaries still living. Contributions have been made over generations, and wisdom has been passed through layers of friends and family. For this reason, there are some special words that I would use on their behalf. You can personalize this to be more appropriate to your family. It can be used during or after the transition.

Privacy

Some people may prefer privacy in their last days—respect that. Maybe they are not interested in the Lawn Bowling team coming to visit once per week or they may not want to video conference with the Veteran's club. There may be a progressive decrease in their desire for company. This is a very intimate time, and interruptions to an internal life review may not be welcomed. Don't take it personally if your friend of 30 years no longer wants to spend time with you. They may have moved on in their spiritual journey while you are still stuck in the physical dramas of the day.

You will have to determine how and when to make contact. You can do this by simply asking "How much company are you looking to have this week?" "Are you interested in seeing Nick from the neighborhood association or should I just give him your regrets for now?" Another way to tell is to look at facial expressions, measure the enthusiasm in the verbal response you get, or monitor how much he is sleeping. Again, we must remember that this is their story. We are there to support, not cause further anxiety.

Caregivers

Support for the caregiver is often overlooked. If this is a family member, they will lose their familiar relationship when the caregiving begins. If you are responsible for your mother's health and well-being, she stops being a mother to you and more of a patient, client, or boarder. You are no longer a daughter, but a chauffeur, cook, nurse, beautician, accountant, and housekeeper. Using the services of a hospice provider or home nursing service allows you to assume some of your family roles again.

The best present a caregiver can receive is time. Offer to sit with the loved one for several hours, allowing the caregiver to work in the garden, get a haircut, or go to the movies. Providing a 'spa day' or restaurant certificate can be a frustrating gift if the caregiver has no time to use it.

A family caregiver has put their life on hold during the illness. It is possible that they left a job, lost contact with friends, temporarily disconnected with their social group, and reduced the amount of time spent with other family members. They cannot grieve because they have to be strong for the dying person and, quite frankly, they have no time to sit and be sad. Many people with a terminal illness will tell me how guilty they feel for all the 'trouble' they have been for their son/daughter/spouse. If you want to provide comfort for the dying, consider what you can do for the caregiver.

Saying Goodbye–Be the friend you would like to have

Be present, consistent, patient, and warm while using a soothing, comforting tone of voice. Offer assurances that you will be there and that you support their transition. Assume that the patient is participating in the conversation even if you can't hear them. They may be speaking in their head, not having the energy to respond physically.

If you would like to help them let go, provide some reassurance that they are not causing pain to others by leaving. Sometimes I hear, "It's OK, you can go now." I suggest that you offer acceptance rather than permission. Say it in a way that is not controlling. "I understand it may be time for you to leave us. I support your decisions. You will always be in our hearts as you move to a higher place." This is a good time to recite or play positive affirmations, reminding them that they are appreciated, loved, and safe.

Death is natural. Our societal frame of reference is what makes it uncomfortable. You don't have to take on the challenges that someone is facing as they approach death. The greatest gift is to simply be there to support their journey. So take your ego out of the room and let love take its place.

CHAPTER 3

— ❧ —

Dying is a Process

*"If you realize that all things change, there is nothing
you will try to hold onto."*

LAO TZU

KNOWING WHAT TO expect as someone is dying will reduce the
mystery and fear of interacting with them. In the past, it was
traditional to move the sick out of sight, perhaps to protect the
living from getting a peek into their own future. But knowing
what to expect can take some of the apprehension out of our
own potential transition and those of the ones we love.

There are many publications and articles that refer to the
physical changes one can expect to see in a person who is dying.
I suggest that if you find yourself in a situation with a life-limiting
illness, do the research into your specific situation. That which
is more difficult to find is a description of what happens to the
person from a spiritual and an emotional viewpoint.

For example, death can be terrifying to someone who has
lived their life on a safe path, avoiding risks and walking away
from challenges. So keep that in mind while you watch your
older sister who is now filled with anxiety, looking apprehensive

about her future. She will need reassurance more than someone who has led a fearless life full of adventure.

Withdrawal

If you or a loved one receive a terminal diagnosis, I encourage you to go out and live your last days together to the fullest extent. A gradual death can be a gift of time—perhaps as much as several months to travel, try new things, or simply visit with the people who are important to you. But there will come a time when you might feel a gradual withdrawal from normal day-to-day activities. Sports or hobbies will no longer be of interest. Grandfather may not want the stimulation of the visits with grandchildren that he used to look forward to. Maybe the nightly news is no longer a ritual that he wants to continue.

In our hospice house, Kayleen was a patient who requested that her curtains stay closed, the lights remain off, and the TV be disconnected. She wanted no visitors, no unnecessary interruptions, and nothing to disturb her concentration. I admired her plan to focus only on her transition, but I wondered why she did not want her family around her at this time. I heard from someone later that she had scheduled a farewell meeting with her family while she was still communicating. She said what she needed to say and then excused them all. They had each (some reluctantly) respected her wishes and had only come back to the room after she had passed.

When you feel that your loved one has begun to withdraw, respect (don't correct) that choice of behavior. It is most likely a sign of acceptance of fate, although it may manifest to you as detachment. It may feel like you have done something wrong, but this is not the case. This is not personal, this is disconnecting from this world in preparation for the next. Gentle support for any change in routine is the best course of action.

Increased Sleeping

Afternoon naps will be a regular occurrence, soon supplemented with morning naps and mid-day naps. The body will become more and more tired to the point where just being awake is exhausting. The spirit uses this time to welcome the presence of those who have gone before, perhaps spending precious moments with a deceased family member who is providing some comfort before the move.

Dreams and waking moments can become mixed, causing confusion for all. Just go with it. It doesn't help anyone to retell a story with a different ending, correct the facts, or to argue about the perceived outcome of an event. As the body prepares itself to shut down, the subconscious mind is becoming more alert and open to the next world. Maintain an environment where this transition is supported; a peaceful setting will ease fatigue for both the dying person and their family.

Visions

Anyone who has had experience with the dying can provide examples of those who have had visions of the previously departed. This can be a direct sighting or it can manifest as eyes wandering around the room apparently following the movements of an unseen entity. It is clear that those who have crossed over can return to accompany those who are about to transition.

Edna had story after story of people, places, and things. We somehow got to Gene Kelly and Donald O'Connor. She talked at length about her experiences with these two famous dancers from the 1940s and 50s. Did she really know them or just remember their performances? She talked about so many friends that it was hard to tell. But her sadness was that "Too many people die young, like me." How old are you?" I asked. "Forty-four," she said. She was really 84. She generally started her conversations with a mischievous smile, like she had a secret she was not going to share. When I served her some pastry, she asked me to cut it into pieces so she could share it with her father (who obviously had passed many years earlier).

Shannon was visiting a friend who was in our hospice with pancreatic cancer. We were talking about how sometimes the dying will see people in the room whom we don't see. She nodded in agreement as she told me a story about the deathbed action of her mother. Her mom had been in a 'sleeping' state for a few days when she suddenly sat up, pointed to the wall, and said, "No Dad I'm not going with you, I'm going with Mom." (Both of her parents were deceased.) After saying that, she promptly fell back into her pillow and proceeded to sleep until the end. Shannon told me that her grandfather had been abusive to the family so she was not surprised that when given the option, her mother chose to leave with her grandmother.

Tess was a beautiful woman in her nineties. She had been one of the original Rosie the Riveter ladies, a proficient ballroom dancer and amateur artist. As she lay dying, she told her daughter about a young boy that had been standing by her bed. He appeared to be about 4 years old with striking blue eyes. By not denying the account, her daughter honored the vision, even though she herself had not seen the child. Later she mentioned to the nurse that her mother had seen this boy. The nurse asked,

"Did he have blond hair?" After the daughter said yes, the nurse explained that a few older women in this facility had seen that very same boy waiting by their bedside. This could be an escort or guide who takes this form of a young boy in order to be seen as non-threatening.

Visions are very real. Because families tend to be stressed at this time, some people make light of these accounts. Do not make a joke of these sightings or try to explain them away using medications or health conditions as an excuse. I ask questions and let the dying person take the lead on how far the discussion will go.

Residential Sightings

Some patients will see visions of people who are not related to them. To me, this is one of the most definitive bits of proof that the sightings are real. The dying are seeing people whom they have never met and can accurately describe them to others.

One patient named Claire asked about the gentlemen who had been sitting on her couch. The nurse looked around and said, "No one has been here." "Oh, yes," she said. "A tall man with gray hair in a flannel shirt was just sitting on my couch. Then he got up and walked out. I don't know who he was." It was a perfect description of Hank, the man who had passed in that room the day before. Two days later, Claire talked about a lady who had come in to her room to say goodbye. "She was short, about my age, wearing a red sweatshirt, and had a silver wig on." Claire went on to tell us what the visitor had said. "*Goodbye, I'm leaving now.*" "I think she must have been someone else's visitor and got the room number wrong, so I wanted to pass the message on to whomever she had meant to see." What she didn't know was that the patient in the next room had passed about ten minutes before her vision. Due to cancer treatments, the lady had lost her hair and always wore a silver wig. And she was definitely the type of person who would stop in and say goodbye to everyone in the hospice house, as she was very social.

Liz, another patient, a young woman in her 40s who had just moved in, told us about an older woman who had been moving ethereally around the room. "There's an old lady who has been flying around the room here. I'm not scared. She seems friendly. But there is something strange about her one eye. It's closed, like she's winking." Liz said. The previous resident of that room had just passed the day before. She was a lady in her 80s who was blind in one eye and had a disfigured eyelid.

Sometimes it is more difficult to identify who the visitor is. I heard of a woman in our facility who said, "There's a little girl sitting on the couch waiting for me." The volunteer asked "Who is she?" The reply was, "I don't know, but she's staying here until I'm ready to leave."

Contact with the Already Departed

Meeting with previously deceased parents and other family members can become more frequent as the terminal illness progresses. Frank was in his mid-eighties and had traveled the world. He had documented his adventures through nearly two dozen photobooks and each week I saw a different part of the world through his eyes. One day as he talked about a cruise that took him around tropical locations in the Gulf of Mexico, he mentioned that his father had come to visit him the day before.

"Did he really?" I smiled. I was intrigued. "Yes," he said "he drove here to pick me up and take me somewhere. I'm not sure where. But he's still driving." Frank laughed and went back to showing me a photo of his favorite restaurant in Cozumel. The next week as we were looking through photos of Arches National Park in Utah, I asked him if his father had been back to see him again. Yes he had. Frank told me that his father must be close to 80 years old by now; I think that—for a brief moment—Frank believed he was in his fifties instead of his eighties. But his father left to go back down to Mississippi to see his mother "She has to be at least 90 by now." In a world without time, I suppose age is not relevant.

Out-of-Body Experiences (OBEs)

As the dying get closer to their last days, it is not uncommon for them to report OBEs. To the uninformed, these experiences are often interpreted as dreams or even hallucinations. A woman I was seeing on a regular basis told me about her sleepless night. "Yes, I couldn't sleep because I had to get to a funeral. When I got there, there were three friends of mine waiting for me. The one told me that I had to get into the . . . you know." She formed a long rectangle with her hands. I took it to mean a coffin. "I did it, but I didn't like it." I nodded for her to continue. "Well I came back from the funeral and tried to move through the house, but Steve (her husband) had blocked all the doors so I couldn't go anywhere. I stayed in bed as long as I could and then I woke him up and told him that I needed to go into the kitchen to get something to eat."

Paulette was clearly having an OBE. This event was so real to her that she truly thought that she had been out of her house, talking to her friends. The conversation she had with her contemporaries was quite clear to her, and she felt that she had total control over her situation until she came back and said the rooms were blocked. This could have been her interpretation of sleep paralysis. When the nurse arrived, Paulette complained of not being able to sleep so they provided medication for her. Unfortunately, this medication will probably dull any future OBEs she may have.

You may also find that as a caregiver, you have become more intuitive. I often hear about family members who have precognitive dreams (or in this case an OBE) about their loved ones.

> *"In a recent OBE, I was downstairs talking to my mother. She began to float up the stairs so I followed her. I thought that maybe she had died and I didn't know what to say to her. So I said "Have a nice transition. Say hi to your sister. . . and Dad. I'm sure they'll meet you there." I was so sure that she would be dead when I woke up that I was totally creeped out. She was alive the next day, but died a few weeks later."*
>
> ELIZA R.

Past Life Bleed-Through

I spoke with Carolyn about her reflections on life. She told me about her family and her thoughts for the short future she had left. And then without missing a beat she said, "I don't know why everybody is killing one another. They're throwing babies overboard, just little babies. Why would anyone do that?" She became upset so I didn't want to push her memories any further. We went into a quiet mode and listened to music.

Another example is a middle-aged woman who was dying from lung cancer. Sarah would wake up in the middle of the night screaming, "We need to get water to the soldiers. The soldiers need water!" She didn't mention this when she saw us in the morning. Naturally we did not bring it up, always waiting for the patient to take the lead on a discussion like this.

Some people are more animated and interested in telling their story. "My friend visited me last night," Richard told me. "I knew him from World War I. I thought he was dead, but he looked pretty good. He didn't like it though, when I told him I thought he was dead." In this life, Richard was not old enough to have been in World War I. In a separate conversation, he told me that his leg had been blown off the previous day. He showed me just above his knee where the explosive made contact. "I was just walking up some stone steps with some other fellas. We were trying to get through a doorway. I don't know where I was and then just like that, it came right through my leg and tore the whole thing off." He gestured to his left leg. He was thankful that 'they' had put him back together for our visit that day.

Because the curtain begins to open as we get closer to death, experiencing bleed-through from a past or future life can generate comments that sound random or illogical to us. Their stories can sound like fantasy, but if we listen closely it is easy to recognize the characteristics of a lucid dream or out-of-body experience. These episodes are very real to the dying, so just follow their lead. If they want to elaborate, they will. If not, let it go.

Feeling the Presence of Another

Sometimes there is just a feeling that a departed soul is still present. There are no visual clues or familiar sounds, but somehow the deceased has brought a sense of being into a room or situation. One such example is a gentleman who had been in our facility for over a year. It was very unusual to have a resident for this period of time and we had all grown fond of him. His name was Ron and when he passed he was missed by many of the staff and volunteers.

Fast forward a few weeks to a female resident, Sandy who was taking her last breaths in the same room where Ron had been for so long. A nurse was telling me about what a nice lady she was. She loved the birds outside of her room and fed them daily. She even named one of them. Sandy had chosen one bird and named him Ron. She had never met the previous patient and there was no discussion of him. This could be a coincidence, but it is more likely that somehow she had received a subliminal message from Ron and had transferred that to her new friend outside the window.

The Desire to Travel

I sat with a family for several months while they cared for their dying father. Liam was a big man who had an interesting life filled with travel, family events, and a notable amount of fund raising for children's charities. His wife of fifty years clearly adored him and his face lit up whenever Debbie came into the room. One day while Debbie was out and I had some time alone with Liam, I tried to reassure him that his journey was just beginning and that he had a beautiful future awaiting him. He had been a little agitated, so I provided some affirmations about being surrounded in love while feeling free and healthy again. I told him that during his travels he would be totally safe and no longer restricted by pain. He was drifting in and out of consciousness and was suffering from some amount of dementia, but he was as clear as anyone I have ever seen when he looked directly at me and asked, "How do you know this for sure?" I told him that many people had been there too early and come back to their current physical condition. They have relayed their accounts through books and interviews, sharing a lot of the same experiences. He replied, "Oh, okay." And then our conversation continued like this:

Liam: Will you help me get my stuff together for the train?

Me: You already have everything you need to get on the train.

Liam: Can I go today?

Me: That is for you to decide. If you think you have finished everything here, then you can go whenever you want to leave.

Liam: Can Debbie go with me?

Me: I don't think so. She still has some work to do here. But she will be on one of those trains right behind you. You will see her as soon as she gets there.

Liam drifted back into a sleepy state, but opened his eyes wide for a moment and said very loudly "Mother!" and then closed his eyes. He did not speak again.

Three Phases of a Spiritual Transition in a Gradual Death

Over time, I have seen some common behaviors in the dying. There seems to be a clear connection between the physical stages of dying and the spiritual progression to the other side. I have documented these stages of transition as they coordinate with physical changes, but remember that dying is different for everyone, so consider these as potential correlations for your loved one.

Realization: The terminally ill are still communicating but perhaps not at the same level as they were when they were in good health. Sometimes this is due to the medication they are receiving, but generally the quality of speech is affected as the disease depletes their energy. Most of their senses are active. They are lethargic but still moving. Even if they are bed-ridden there is still some muscle function. This is the time when people begin to talk about events in their life, confirming that their loved ones are in positive situations. Did Jack Jr. graduate yet? How does Jessica like her new job? They probably know that they are dying, but they may not want to verbalize it to protect the feelings of their loved ones. I rarely see any outward indications of fear.

You might hear travel metaphors such as, "I need to pack." Or, "I have to catch the bus soon." One of my patients pointed to some items in his room, telling me that he needed to put those things in the car. Another woke just long enough to ask, "Do you know where Connelly Street is?" I told him I could find it if I had a map. He then asked, "Would you drive me there?" I told him that it was likely that he would be able to drive himself there soon. To us, it sounds nonsensical; but to them it is very real. We should not question or correct their statements.

They are thanking people for their help, saying 'I love you' to friends and family, and maybe showing some emotion when visitors come and go. This is the beginning of relationship closure. I see some sadness as they realize that their time has become very limited. You might see some renewal of religious practice (saying the rosary, a preference for gospel music, reciting from a holy book, etc.) Because there is still mindful activity, this is a great time to talk through any unresolved issues, thanking them for being in your life, or confirming that they had a meaningful time on Earth.

Review: One by one, the senses become disabled. Food is no longer welcomed and talking stops. The arms and legs are so tired, they can barely move, if at all. You might get a hand squeeze, or see some muscle jerks around the feet. Eye movements no longer follow the physical people in the room but they may see people who have previously passed away. If they are still talking, they may tell you about their visitors, generally friends or family who have already passed to the other side. We know that the dying communicate with those who will meet them at the end. At this point they are beginning to free their hold on the physical world. Their spirit is gradually being reintroduced to the astral world to mitigate an abrupt change. This is the one-foot-in / one-foot-out scenario we have heard about from end-of-life professionals. Your presence is still felt, even if not acknowledged.

Release: Now the dying person goes into full-sleep mode. Eyes may stay open or be closed with some fluttering. There is no longer any speech, physical movement, or recognition that anyone is in the room. Their hearing may still be selectively on and off. I always assume that it is on. Breathing becomes labored, almost as an afterthought. This is the time period in which the spirit is looking over the physical existence. They are taking inventory of their life, perhaps counting the wins, regretting some of the losses. You might see furrowed brows, smiles for no apparent reason, and an occasional sigh.

Affirmations of forgiveness are very meaningful at this time, as the dying will examine some of the perceived 'mistakes' that they believe they made. They know it is almost time to go and they are developing the courage to make the final steps into the next world.

I sat with a woman who was near death. Her breathing was slow, her eyes were closed, and she had no movement in her body at all. Her granddaughter was there and gazed upon her with such love and devotion that I had to ask about her grandmother's life. Alice had been born in Estonia and lived a quiet country life. That is until World War II. The family had made plans to escape; she would go to Germany and her sister would follow the next day. While Alice ended up in a German refugee camp, her sister was captured by the Russians and taken to Siberia. Each sibling did not know what had happened to the other. After being released from the camp, Alice was able to get on a boat and sail to the U.S.

She landed in New York City as did so many others, without knowing any English or having any money. The local Estonian community took her in and she eventually married and had a daughter of her own. Alice and her husband had a good life until a few years ago when he died. She moved to Delaware to be with her daughter's family. And now here she was taking her last breaths. The family was surprised that she had been like this for almost a week. They wondered why she was 'holding on' for so many days. At this point Alice was preparing to release. In her physical life, every time she made a move it was filled with fear and she was heartbroken at the loss of what she was leaving behind. You can imagine that it would take some time for her to work up the courage to make this final move. It was apparent by her facial expression that her spirit was in the midst of some tough decisions before she would be ready to transition.

By the way, you will be happy to know that sometime in the 1980s she had been able to reconnect with her sister, who had been released at some point and had returned to their Estonian country home. At the time of this writing, Alice, her sister, and her husband are most likely together again.

Recognizing Special Moments

We all have our theories of what sights, sounds, symbols, and smells might mean during any traumatic, stressful time in our life. It is up to us to interpret these in a way that helps us to make it through. There is no right or wrong answer.

I was consoling a woman who had been visiting her mother in our hospice care facility. Lynda had tears in her eyes and was talking about how well the nurses were taking care of her mother as she lay dying. Just then she looked away and said, "Do you smell that? It's like roses. I don't see any around here." She continued with her story, occasionally dabbing a tissue to the corner of her eye. "Oh, there it is again. You don't smell that?" I really wish I had, but honestly I didn't smell anything. I asked her if roses held any special place in the family. At first she shook her head and said she couldn't think of anything. She began to tell me about her living sister and the recent health issues she had. They wanted their mother to stay at home but couldn't physically handle the responsibility. At that moment, she perked up and said, "There it is again. That rose smell." She turned to me and said, "You know my aunt and uncle had prize rose bushes. They were very well known in the area for their gardens. One rose that they cross-bred was even named after my uncle." I asked if they had passed. When she said yes, they had both died about one year previously; I knew why she smelled the roses. I said, "Maybe they are here to help your mom make the transition. This could be a sign from them." I hoped that I could make her feel more comfortable with that thought.

When I tell people what I do as a volunteer, I often hear the response, and "How could you do that? It must be so hard." Or, "I could never do that." I have always felt it to be an honor to be a part of someone's transition. This is by far the most important endeavor of this lifetime and they are allowing me to share it with them. If you have a chance to do this with your loved one, use the information in this book to make the most of the experience, both for you and for them.

CHAPTER 4

───── ❧ ─────

Support a Peaceful Crossing

"Use what talents you possess. The woods would be very silent if no birds sang except those that sang best. "

HENRY VAN DYKE

Reiki in Hospice

ALTHOUGH ROOTED IN ancient Tibetan teachings, Reiki was rediscovered in the mid-1800s by Dr. Mikao Usui, a Japanese monk/educator. In a hospice setting, this technique is used for stress reduction and relaxation. Life-force energy that naturally flows through us can be low or weak, especially during an illness or injury. A process of using hand positions around the client/patient's body by a trained and certified practitioner is designed to raise the energy level and promote feelings of health and peace. More information can be found on the resource pages in the back of this book.

When Bill was diagnosed with cancer and faced many pain-filled days and nights, I researched what I could do to help him. I found Reiki and together we employed the techniques to help eliminate some of his discomfort and speed the healing process. I went on to receive my master certification and decided to use it in my volunteer work with hospice patients. Because it is not yet a mainstream practice, I was hesitant to talk about it with my colleagues. I find now that more and more medical professionals are embracing the process as a complement to their practice. My hospice intake group offers this service to all incoming patients and this is where I receive my requests. Most of my patient families have not heard of Reiki, but are willing to try anything that would bring a feeling of ease to their loved one. Inviting the staff and families in to witness the techniques takes away the mystery and shows how special these moments can be.

"As soon as Reiki is activated, its high frequencies of energy immediately begin to raise our vibration, activate our spiritual guidance and increase our life force energy."

COLLEEN BENELLI

I frequently use Reiki as a tool to assist with relaxation both at the facilities and in homes. As the medical staff has been educated about this service, they will sometimes make recommendations to me. If a patient is restless, sad, or uncomfortable, they will ask me to stop in and provide a Reiki session. Because of the logistics of a hospital bed and other medical equipment, the hand positions and timing are modified to fit the situation. The door is shut and music plays softly in the background. I invite the family to stay if they would like and generally it becomes a very special, sacred time for whoever is in the room.

I start with introductions and a request for permission to be there. Gratitude is always part of my introduction as I thank the patient and/or family for inviting me to be a part of this significant time in their life. This is heartfelt, because I truly feel blessed to be included in this event. It is a gift to me.

So I might begin like this.

"Hello, Sarina. My name is Susan and I am here to help you relax and send some healing energy to you. First, I would like to thank you and your family for allowing me to be a part of this incredible journey that you are taking. If it is OK with you, I would now like to invite my Reiki guides to support us. And anyone in the room who is here for Sarina, please assist me in bringing light and peace to this beautiful soul."

I cannot think of a single time that I have done this and not felt a tremendous amount of positive energy in the room. There are swirls of power that float in and through my body. I am certain that when I ask for assistance from my guides, the spiritual helpers of the dying, and those souls who have passed before, they are all there and jumping around the room to assist. The hairs on my arms and neck stand up and I have chills and surges of complete joy. My chakras are open and spinning wildly, and the love that is present cannot be described in words.

At this point I begin moving around the bed and placing my hands wherever I can reach or where I feel that the warmth is needed. One of my home patients requested a treatment and he felt so at peace when we were finished that his wife asked me for a session. During my next visit, I worked with her first and she was giddy that her knees didn't hurt for the first time in weeks. On subsequent visits, I think she got more relief than he did. The stress on her as a caregiver was quite substantial, and

I believe that her anxiety manifested as pain in several areas of her body. I was glad to be able to help her relax.

I also use the Reiki precepts in some of my sessions. Again, modified to fit the situation, I reference the person's life.

Just for today:

- *I will not be angry*
- *I will not worry*
- *I will give thanks for my many blessings*
- *I will do my work honestly*
- *I will be kind to my neighbor and every living thing*

There is some good information available about the impact of Reiki on the very sick. An excellent book on the subject is <u>Reiki Energy Medicine: Bringing Healing Touch into Home, Hospital and Hospice</u>. This text written by Libby Barnett and Maggie Babb explains the impact of the energy field on the body's healing systems. I have studied under Maggie, and she demonstrates a tender, caring approach to in-hospice Reiki for patients, families, and even staff.

Journaling

Journaling to document feelings and events can be an effective tool for both the dying and their supporting team. There are so many issues on our minds when we are coming to terms with life and death. If a professional counselor is available to you, I recommend taking that opportunity, but many times you would rather explore your own feelings. Or maybe the timing is not right to speak to anyone; it could be midnight as you sit bedside in a hospice room. Writing can be a good way to put into words any of the emotions you have trouble showing or sharing. It can also identify unresolved issues and allow you to address them.

Pet Therapy

My friend, and fellow volunteer, has a sociable golden doodle dog that visits our facility every Sunday morning. Lady is very gentle and truly loves her 'job' as companion, entertainer, and foot licker. Yes, that's right; we had one gentleman who loved to have his feet licked. He started to lose track of time but always knew when it was Sunday, because that's when his four-legged friend would come by to see him. The right animal can have a very calming effect on someone who is facing death. Most people have a fond remembrance of a family or neighborhood pet. And so it becomes a pleasant part of their life review. Naturally, we always ask permission before entering a room. Not everyone has the same warm feelings about dogs and cats.

Some facilities also allow family pets to visit on a limited basis. This is a nod to keeping their lives as normal as possible.

At home, families should do what makes them comfortable regarding their pets. If the pet parent is used to having the dog or cat in bed with them, then why not allow it now? Animals have instincts about their owner's health. I believe it helps to comfort them both.

Meditation and Guided Imagery

I created this passage one evening as I watched someone seemingly struggle with their transition. I thought about what it might look like to cross into the next world and what I would want to hear to motivate me to take that next step.

Crossing the Bridge

You are lying down because you are very tired. It is a little chilly and your muscles are achy. Your eyelids are very heavy and all you want to do is sleep. But something in the distance is calling you. You can barely hear it; voices are calling your name. Even though you are tired, you decide to get up and follow the sounds. You rise from your bed and begin with a few small steps. A path becomes clear so you start to walk along the trail. Your legs are heavy, but with each step the music becomes louder and you are very curious about it. Step by step, you begin to feel more energy. You continue down the path and your muscles are becoming stronger and stronger. You feel yourself moving a little bit faster now. The chill is gone and you are warm, full of energy. In the distance there is a golden glow. You can't stop looking at it, and you walk faster toward this beautiful, radiant warmth. The voices are becoming louder, as you hear your name being called again. The music is becoming clear now, and there is laughter. You are walking faster and faster down the path as your energy continues to increase. You are lighter and lighter, with no cares, no worries. All is forgiven. You only have good, positive feelings for yourself and all others. As you continue on the path, it becomes clear that there is a bridge you must cross to reach the music and people. This is the bridge that will connect you to your higher self. You slow down, hesitate. The bridge crosses an abyss and you can't see the bottom. Somehow you know that once you go over the bridge, there will be no turning back. The music continues, your name is called again, and you decide to complete your journey. Your pace picks back up and you walk briskly onto the bridge. You are so light that you can barely feel your feet hit the ground. You are halfway across and you know you have made the right decision. There are faces on the other side that you recognize. The laughter and music are louder, people are dancing. As you finish crossing, the golden glow surrounds you, warms you to the bone. You are so comfortable. You know you have reached a place of love and peace; your higher self has returned home.

Continuing with soft music might be a comforting addition to this visualization. Affirmations playing after this script can also continue the theme of moving on to your higher self.

Physical Changes

Some of the physical changes that I have seen in patients who have been exposed to complementary care techniques confirm that there is a positive impact from the relaxation. When you can stop all of the extraneous activity surrounding them, relieve pain and reduce fear, people seem to focus better on their spiritual objectives. Here are some examples:

- A man with brain cancer lay unresponsive with his arms held tightly to his chest and his hands clenched as though trying to hold onto something. After a Reiki session, his arms relaxed and he let his hands loose so that his wife could hold them in hers.

- Gasping for air and snoring loudly, a woman with breast cancer tried to sleep but was constantly interrupted by her own breathing difficulties. I could tell that every breath was a struggle for her. As we listened to some music that included water and other nature sounds, I quietly recited some *Destination: Higher Self* audio CD affirmations to her. After about five minutes, her breathing became easier and her brow relaxed. She had found a clear way to move oxygen through her body.

- A Reiki session on a caregiver's knees allowed her to move more easily through the apartment. She was very grateful because now it was not so painful to care for her dying husband.

- His ALS had left him unable to move any part of his body except for his head. Once a week I would travel to his home and with a soft Hemi-Sync® music background, I gently massaged his feet. His caregiver told me it was the highlight of his week—the only time that he could stop thinking about his illness and quietly meditate. This was particularly meaningful when I learned that this disease had caused him to have constant muscle pain. His caregiver could not understand why the healing touch techniques were not causing him discomfort, but he actually looked forward to the visit.

- A man with HIV had severe back pain that was not relieved by drugs. After a few minutes of Reiki, he was moaning with relief as his muscles began to unwind.

- A woman was dying in an assisted-living home. Due to her age, she had few living relatives and they were elderly as well. She was noticeably frightened as she rocked back and forth in a chair, quietly saying "help me." With some music and affirmations, I held her until she could sleep peacefully. Her face showed a visible release of apprehension.

- A combination of ALS and a degenerative bone disease had a middle aged woman in constant pain. Medications weren't working due to her high stress level and severe anxiety. After a session of low lights, caring touch, music and simple affirmations, she became very relaxed – napping for the first time in weeks. Her body allowed the morphine to work as soon as the tension was released from her muscles.

- After a quiet visualization accompanied by music, an elderly man began to shed happy tears as he told me that he was ready to go now.

- One gentleman who had been very depressed was cheered every time our therapy dog came in to see him. He told me later that it reminded him that he would see his own beloved pet soon and it gave him something positive to think about, as he knew he was dying.

Remember the point of this is to release the pain and tension from the body so that the emotional gates can open. This is a powerful assist to achieving your spiritual goals and connecting with your higher self.

Life-Review Triggers

When I am sitting with the dying and their families, I find that asking questions about their lives is a good way to elevate a somber mood because it focuses them on celebrating their lives.

One question can often lead to another. Generally, I hear good stories, moments of family pride, and reflections of a lifetime with meaning. I believe this also begins to trigger a life review for everyone else in the room if they haven't already thought about it. Be aware that not everyone wants to talk and that's OK. You don't want to appear as if you are conducting a survey or prying into their personal business.

Here are some of the questions I use if the patient is aware, responsive, and in a talking mood:

"How did you two meet?" (This is in reference to a photo of a spouse or partner.)

"Have you traveled anywhere special?"

"Tell me about this photo/your children/the handmade quilt on your bed."

"What was your first car like?"

"What was your first job?"

"Did you grow up in this area? Tell me about other places you have lived."

"What changes have you seen in the last 10/20/30 years that have impressed you the most?"

If the patient is sleeping, but listening, I might ask the family members these questions, always being aware that the loved one can likely hear the conversation:

"What was your grandmother's life like? Was she a good cook?"

"What is your favorite holiday memory?"

"What is the most important lesson you have learned from your mother?"

"What do you remember most about your childhood?"

"Did you have any adventures with your brother when you were kids?"

"What is your sister's favorite hobby/TV show/movie?"

"Tell me about a favorite memory that you have of your father."

Once I asked an older gentleman how many presidents he had seen in his lifetime. His response was, "All of them." We had a nice laugh from that answer.

In a home setting, life reviews can also be done through photo albums, collections, and documents (diplomas, certificates, etc.) Allow the family to take the lead so as not to appear that you are assessing their belongings.

Top Ten Conditions that Impede a Peaceful Transition

After watching hundreds of patients and their interactions with friends and family in the care of hospice, I have observed some common situations in which spiritual evolution is hindered. Here is a summary of what you can do to make the most of your home or hospice experience and that will ultimately support a peaceful transition.

1. **People talking about the patient as though they were not in the room.** This includes medical information as well as future planning. Especially disturbing are the families who talk about dividing assets, funeral planning, or personal inconveniences before the last breath is even taken. Confine your conversations to calming, peaceful, and loving thoughts for the dying. The dying can hear you.

2. **Withholding pain medication for fear of addiction or desertion.** When asked why she was so hesitant to provide

pain meds to her distressed husband of sixty years, Netta's response was, "That way I can tell he's still alive, still with me." Medication is for the comfort of the dying. It is selfish to withhold it to satisfy your own needs. Consider the directions given by your medical team, as they have plenty of experience in this field.

3. **Keeping the TV or radio on for diversion.** Silence can be uncomfortable for loved ones but could be soothing for a troubled mind. Listening to game shows hour after hour will do nothing to assist a dying person in their life review and journey of consciousness. Soft music is a better alternative than a constant barrage of world news or reality shows.

4. **Displaying religious items that were not a recent part of their life.** If someone was not deeply religious during their active life, then it can be confusing to hear gospel music, feel rosary beads around their hands, or see religious statues in their line of vision. Items from nature are neutral and might be more relaxing.

5. **Feeding the terminal patient after the medical team has advised against it.** There are physical reasons to stop food and drink for a dying person. You think you are helping by providing water to your loved one, but could be causing more harm. Always follow the direction of your medical resources. Ice chips and wet mouth sponges can relieve dry mouth without creating a choking hazard.

6. **Overstimulating someone with a constant stream of visitors, unrelated chit-chat, and/or unnecessary noises.** Your loved one may feel obligated to stay awake, answer questions, or entertain visitors even as they lie exhausted. Instead you might consider having one last farewell event when your father can still communicate reasonably

well and then ask everyone to give their regards through prayer and good wishes from home.

7. **Encouraging the patient to fight a terminal disease.** Once a terminal illness has been diagnosed and all other methods of cure have been exhausted, it is time for all concerned to accept the inevitable. Can you pray for a miracle? Sure, but to tell your mother to 'Stay tough,' 'Hang in there,' 'You can beat this thing,' or 'Keep fighting' is to put a challenge in front of her that she cannot win. Denial will not help. It is more supportive to find out what she will need to transition without regrets and do what it takes to help her achieve that goal.

8. **Loud crying, lamenting, or otherwise creating an environment of heavy grief.** This extreme emotion can create an attachment that holds the dying to the physical realm. Sobbing and groaning can make the dying feel guilty for leaving you this way. Placing or taking blame for the disease or other sad conditions are also not productive. If you are overwhelmed by grief and cannot help but show it, leave the room and get out of the dying person's hearing range. Many cultures understand this and perform joyful celebrations of the person's life.

9. **Clutter in the sacred space.** Having medical equipment, cleaning supplies and personal-care items in their line of vision is a constant reminder of the disease and another tie to the physical world. Move clutter to an area that is not visible to the dying.

10. **Trying to manipulate the natural timeline.** You cannot rush or delay someone's dying with your wishes. People will die on their own schedule. If it is taking too long in your mind, then it is possible that your loved one has more spiritual work

to do before their heart beats for the last time. If it seems to move too fast, then celebrate the joyful return home of their soul. Always remember: it is their journey—not yours.

Whether you are using the services of a medical facility or caring for your loved one independently, please consider these points when providing end of life support.

Many of these therapies and care strategies are available through hospice organizations. The purpose is to provide comfort and support for the dying and their families. As the medical team focuses on pain management, nutrition, and other physical requirements of the patient, a group of volunteers can provide extra services that support spiritual, emotional and intellectual needs. If you or a loved one is diagnosed with a life-limiting illness, I highly recommend enlisting the services of a hospice provider.

> *"I have expressed again and again my admiration for the pioneering work that is being done in the hospice movement. In it at last we see the dying being treated with the dignity they deserve. I would like here to make a deep plea to all the governments of the world that they should encourage the creation of hospices and fund them as generously as possible."*

> SOGYAL RINPOCHE
> THE TIBETAN BOOK OF LIVING AND DYING

CHAPTER 5

The Doula: An End-of-Life Companion

"Never worry about numbers. Help one person at a time, and always start with the person nearest you."

MOTHER TERESA

NOT EVERYONE IS equipped to handle all of the activities that accompany a life-limiting illness. Whether or not you choose to use the services of a hospice organization, you might consider securing the assistance of a doula when the end becomes near.

An end-of-life doula is a companion to the actively dying. Other terms are 11th hour volunteer, transition coach, and end-of-life coach. This person (or team) is generally not a medical professional, but a trusted member of your faith based organization, a volunteer from hospice or other medical facility, or even a family friend. There is some very specific training provided by hospice organizations if you want to pursue this as a volunteer. However, if you have a family member who could benefit from this type of help and you want to provide it, I have listed some of the main duties below. The primary purpose of a doula is to provide comfort and companionship to the dying, but they can also be a liaison between the family and the medical team if required.

There are professional doulas that charge monetary fees. Services run the gamut from house visits and companionship to home funerals and ceremonial assistance. At the time of this writing, there were no state certifications for this service, although there are many independent organizations that provide training. Therefore, I recommend that you conduct your own thorough research prior to making a selection. (I have provided a few organizations in the resource section as examples only.) The description below is primarily that of a hospice volunteer. If you choose to hire someone for this task, you can specify exactly what you would like them to do and agree on the cost up front.

Role of a Doula

Why would you want a doula at your bedside during your transition? There are a number of benefits. A doula can have a calming presence during an emotionally charged time. Death creates tension in our society and a neutral party can temper some of that stress. Most doulas have been trained in the details of dying and can provide some instruction to the dying person's loved ones. But one of the most important functions of an end-of-life coach is to provide emotional (and sometimes spiritual) support to the dying.

The Dying Process

A doula must be familiar with the physical aspects of the dying process. One of my friends on our doula team told me the story of a family that requested her services because although they did not want their family member to be alone, everyone there was afraid to be in the same room with their dying father. They had such fear of the actual death that they could not provide the support that their family member so desperately needed. As a matter of fact, they did not even want to go through the room to get to another area of the house. This created a very low emotional frequency in the home and became a missed opportunity to help their loved one reach their highest spiritual level during transition. A doula can educate the uninformed about the dying process to remove the negative emotions associated with uncertainty. Then the family can focus on unconditional love and in doing so the overall vibration will increase.

Patience

Every death is different. Our doula team has been in the situation where we will sit with a patient for days after everyone thought the transition was imminent. When I first began serving as a doula, I would sit with the dying person thinking, "Now that I'm here, the last breath should be coming at any moment." I needed to learn that this is all about the dying person, not about me as a doula. Maintain respect for the dying as this is the ultimate support role. People will die when they are ready and not a moment before.

There was a resident named Holly who was uncomfortable, unable to speak due to a stroke earlier that summer. She had difficulty in breathing and continued to grab at the covers. On Sunday morning, I had a Reiki session with her. Her face began to soften as she seemed to relax. Her daughter spoke about her life at length. Her mother was 91 and had been widowed for 39 years. Up until two years earlier, she had lived by herself without a driver's license, taking the bus everywhere from church to the store. When her daughter retired, she began to drive her around. She was very sad about her mother's condition, fearing that maybe she had pushed her too far and caused the stroke. I returned on Monday morning to see how Holly was doing and met her daughter in the hall. She had tears in eyes and said, "She's gone. She died earlier this morning." I told her how sorry I was for her loss. She encouraged me to go in to the room where Holly (by that I mean Holly's body) was still in her bed. The son and grandson were in the room apparently waiting for the funeral home to come. We talked again about the remarkable life Holly had led and how much change she had seen in her lifetime. Holly's daughter felt bad. "I've been here for days, sleeping on the couch. Last night I tried to stay awake, but I just couldn't do it any longer and closed my eyes. When I woke up, I saw that she was no longer breathing. I called the nurse and she verified it with a stethoscope." I told her, "Maybe she had waited for you to sleep, so you wouldn't see her transition. The important thing is that you were there for her and she knew it." There are a number of stories suggesting that many of the dying will wait until they are alone to take their final breath.

As we waited for the funeral team to arrive, I told the family that I felt that her spirit was still there and they could celebrate her life. We talked about her childhood growing up as the daughter of a bricklayer and how strong she had been as she lived for almost forty years as a single woman in the city. Her generation had lived through many hardships, but she had overcome the tough times and thrived into her 90s. The daughter seemed more comfortable about having missed Holly's last breath. She redirected her thoughts to honor the years she had spent with her rather than mourn the one moment she had missed.

Keep an Open Mind

Another crucial skill is to be nonjudgmental. Between family dramas, religious preferences, cultural practices, and even economic situations, you are likely to find yourself in the middle of things you don't understand or agree with. Again, this requires respect for the dying. Your role is to be a neutral and calming influence. To do this, you must remain composed and not join in the controversial discussions that may pop up. Listen to what is being said and try to accommodate without interfering. Ask questions that could lead to conflict resolution. For example, "Burning incense is a lovely idea. Can we gain the same impact if we do it in the next room so Aunt Peg's eyes don't burn?" or, "A dark room would be very comforting for your grandmother. Maybe we could put some soft lights on the floor under the bed, so Uncle John doesn't trip on the nightstand." You get the idea. If the topic is not something you want to be involved in, simply ask the family if they could move their meeting to another room so Pop can rest.

Availability

Because people will die on their own schedule, yours must be somewhat flexible. Some hospice facilities have doula schedules so that you know, for example, that every second and fourth Thursday you will be at the facility to cover whatever need should arise. Other times, we are called when a family requests us. Perhaps there is an event such as a wedding or birthday that everyone would like to attend. In that case, a doula can be assigned to ensure that if the time comes, the patient does not die alone. Sometimes there's not much time to prepare. I recently was called in to relieve a grandson who was exhausted after spending several days with his grandmother. He wanted to go home, take a shower, get a change of clothes, and return after a brief nap. As you would know it, I was not there for very long when Grandma stopped breathing. The nurse confirmed it with several pulse checks and a stethoscope. She was pronounced dead only 30 minutes after he had left. I sat with her until he returned so that she would not be alone. Providing some affirmations, I encouraged her to seek the highest plane that was appropriate. When her grandson arrived, I helped him pack her things while the nurse called the funeral director. This is a case in which I spent more time with the patient after her last breath than before.

Religious Assumptions

A doula should not impose their own religious views on the patient nor should they make assumptions about the household. If time permits, you may want to do some research on the family's choices. This is not so you can lead religious ceremonies, but so you can be more understanding of those who will. In our hospice house, the local scout troops were decking the halls for the Christmas holidays. The family I was with was adamant about not having a wreath on the door. I assumed it was because they were not in a festive mood—understandable, given the circumstances. The next day there was a menorah on the dresser. They were Jewish.

Support the Family

The most important attribute of a successful doula is the ability to make the family feel at ease. Encourage family stories and review photos; talk about hobbies or any organizations that their loved one was involved with. Celebrate their life as opposed to grieving their death. One of my favorite experiences was a 90-year-old war hero (a bronze star recipient, his family bragged to me). When I met him he was already actively dying. With eyes that didn't blink and a slow steady rasping breath, I knew that he had only days to live—maybe less. His lovely wife of over 65 years grabbed me the moment I walked through the door. She sobbed loudly, her grief apparent. She gathered herself and sat beside him, holding his hand as though she could transfer some of her life to him. "I think he can get better," she said. "Doctors don't always know." I asked about the man in the bed who was so obviously loved by his family. He worked with professional boxers, knew Joe Louis from Detroit. I heard stories about his impact on the boxing profession and his connection to Hulk Hogan. His wife cried as she talked about his war stories—he was in the Navy aboard the USS Saratoga. I could see the pride that they all had in him. Although the family grieved, talking about his experiences helped to ease the heaviness in the room as they shared their love for him. And knowing that he could hear every word they said, I am sure it was confirmation for him that he had lived an accomplished life and that his family loved him very much.

I sat with Juanita for an hour or two and prayed that she was finding her way to a new world, one in which she could breathe more easily and have the energy to pursue her dreams. Her son, Jerome, quickly walked in while I was whispering to her. "I was at work," he said, breathless, "but I couldn't concentrate—my head was here. I know I have to be at her side right now." I began to rise and he stopped me, asking that we pray together. I continued my affirmations for a few minutes and then raised my head. He walked over and gave me a bear hug—not the kind where you briefly touch shoulders and provide an obligatory pat on the back, but a sincere embrace. "Thank you so much for being with her while I wasn't. I can't tell you how important it is to know she hasn't been alone." This athletic, six-foot-tall man wiped a tear from his eye as he said it.

And that's why I do it.

CHAPTER 6

─── ✦ ───

A Sacred Space and Time

"Death is no more than passing from one room into another. But there is a difference for me, you know. In that other room I shall be able to see."

HELEN KELLER

A SACRED SPACE can be set up in your home, in a medical facility, or wherever your group has decided to share the last few days or hours. Many people say they would prefer to spend their end of days with family in their home, while others prefer the quiet space of a facility that is designed for care of the dying. If finances allow, maybe your dying grandfather would like to travel back to his hometown to be surrounded by familiar sites. Wherever this occurs, think about some of the following key points. The recurring theme is to honor the soul who is about to make the transition.

Respect the Time

Always show reverence for the moment. No matter what might be happening in your life, the most important thing is to focus on the person who is in transition. They need to be at peace surrounded only by love and support.

What struck me about Reba right away was her affinity for telling the truth. If she didn't like a meal, she would say it. Not in a mean way, but just to let the staff know that a particular recipe was not a winner. She was on dialysis three times per week and wheeled herself around to visit other residents. They appreciated her visits. She was bored and wasn't really sure what was next in her life—perhaps she was in limbo waiting for something to happen. I saw her visiting another resident on Friday, but by the following Tuesday she was in bed frail and sleepy. I sat with her only son for a while and talked about what a sweet lady she is. (Not *was*, because I know she could hear us and I didn't want to talk in the past tense.) I commented on her beautiful skin, the Christmas tree that was brightly decorated in the corner of her room, and the handmade quilt adorning the foot of her bed. I came back on Wednesday and saw that she had gotten weaker. She had the classic signs of beginning her transition. Her eyes were open and not blinking, her breathing was labored and open-mouthed. She was not speaking, but I could see that she was hearing us. This is when I met her daughter, Jasmine. She talked quite profusely about everything going on in her life (cats, birth order of her siblings, raising goats, husband's motorcycle, life on the farm, and well, you get the picture.) At first I thought this was nervous energy. Based on her comments about death and spirituality, I thought she might be open for a Reiki session for her mother. When I offered, she was very enthusiastic. I had already scheduled a session for the resident across the hall but assured her that I would be back in about 40 minutes.

When I returned there was so much non-physical presence in the room; I felt multiple energies surrounding me, other souls waiting to accompany Reba home. Meanwhile, Jasmine's friend had joined us. They were excited to tell me about their psychic friend and photographs with orbs. They needed to assure me that they were very 'new age' (even if their husbands were not in synch with them). I began the session peacefully, but it was only a few minutes before they started quietly gossiping back and forth to each other on totally unrelated topics. Then a cell phone rang and it was answered in loud whispers. During the entire session, these two were gabbing about all the 'drama' in their lives. I thought about stopping, but it was her mother—she had a right to respond as she saw fit. Not only that, but I felt that higher energy was still getting through. When I was done, they thanked me, told me how beautiful it was, and said they thought it was bringing their mother some peace. I just wanted to spend some time alone with Reba, but I have to be careful that I don't take over the spiritual care of someone else's loved one.

During my next session with another patient, I led with, "I'd like to ask you to silence your cell phones and please help Tony focus by keeping as quiet as possible." Generally people do— they stand in prayer while I'm doing my session. But I know I can't always depend on it.

I was sitting as a doula for Millie, one of my hospice residents, as her breath slowed to about three or four times per minute. I held her hand and we listened to soft music in the background. A man entered the room, escorting the dying woman's sister in a wheelchair. I rose to give the family some privacy. In a loud voice, the man told me, "Don't worry about it. We know she's dying. We all die." I guess my facial expression said it all, so he responded with, "She never liked me anyway, so there's no need to be nice to her now." And of course as I exited the room I heard, "Oh man it stinks in here!" This is an extreme situation, but it provides an example of how people can be insensitive about the dying process. I said to the nurse on my way out, "Someday he'll be in this situation, and only then will he realize what he has done today."

Cleanliness of the Space and the Body

One of the concerns of the dying as they begin to lose control of their body and their environment is cleanliness. During the course of the day, most of us use deodorant, brush our teeth, and keep our hair clean and combed. This is a luxury to someone in a weakened condition. Helping someone to stay clean and fresh is a wonderful gift. Using a soft, warm cloth to gently wipe the face, hands, and feet can be very soothing. Many of the ladies I see in hospice have their nails painted, their hair combed, and sometimes they are even wearing lipstick. This brings some normalcy along with the statement, "I am still a person. Don't forget me. I still have feelings and desires." Changing the bed linens is comforting. Having the floors swept and the surfaces free of debris (old newspapers, coffee cups, etc.) shows respect. Remove dead flowers, keep the trash bins emptied, and if possible open a window to keep the air circulating.

Basics of Creating the Sacred Space

We can't always pick when and where a person will die, so there is not always an opportunity to provide all of the considerations listed below, but we can develop a sacred feeling wherever the transition occurs. A space can be created even if there are only hours left in life. You can establish an atmosphere of love and peace even in a hospital setting if it is thoughtfully planned. In the Buddhist philosophy, the space around the dying should be free of all things that would draw attention away from the mission. Items such as photographs and other material possessions can keep the spirit attached to the physical world. This is something to consider as you develop your space.

If you have the ability to choose, select an area that is free of excess noise and traffic. You should be able to play soft music and welcome guests. These are all good discussion points and can be part of your Spiritual Directive planning.

Clearing and Blessing the Space

Many people find comfort in burning sage in the space to clear any negative energy that might be lingering. As always, be sure you are in an area that is ventilated and does not prohibit open flame (such as where oxygen is in use.) This is a sample of an opening prayer that can be used. It is appropriate whether the dying person is present or has yet to be settled in. Begin with a moment of silence that allows all participants to clear their minds and welcome guides for assistance.

"As we prepare this space for the sacred transition of our cousin Ben, we ask for God's blessing. Positive energy and expressions are welcome here. This is a safe and loving place. We invite all of our guides to participate as we celebrate the end of Ben's earthly

journey and the beginning of his transition to the next level of his spiritual evolution. Everything in this space is here to support this profound event."

Follow this with some affirmations and personal messages if desired. Use your intuition to guide your words.

Notification

Let people know that you have created a sacred space and what the expectations are. Ask them to turn their cell phones off (or leave them at the door to keep temptation at bay).

"Ben is transitioning. We would like for you to respect the space while you share your love and memories. We invite you to wish Ben well on his journey and provide positive encouragement to him. Thank you for sharing this time with him."

Altar

Any flat surface can become an altar. A bench, table, or shelf can be made into a sacred place for display of personal items. You can include natural objects such as stones from a local hiking path, sand from a favorite beach, or feathers found near a backyard bird house—anything that has special meaning to the dying person. Personal items that represent or symbolize their highest spiritual goal or intention might be appropriate. The important note here is to keep these items to a minimum. Do not clutter the space or have too many items that would induce the desire to focus on the physical world.

Candles

First and most important is safety. Do not use any flame-based lighting while oxygen is in use. Always be sure to have an alert adult in the room if candles are part of your plan. Follow any directions that are posted on the packaging. Consider the many varieties of battery-operated candles that are available today. These are not hazardous and still provide nice ambient lighting. Pink light bulbs in a small lamp also cast a soft, warm glow. (Unless it is medically necessary, harsh overhead or fluorescent lights should not be a part of the lighting plan.)

Color

Color can be very soothing or somewhat stimulating. Which do you prefer? Maybe colors that are associated with the chakras would be your choice. Or something that is a reflection of nature would make you happy. Perhaps pure white is the best. Whatever it is, make it right for whoever is dying—not what you think others would like. Use the color choices for bedding, lighting, clothing, flowers, and/or artwork.

Crystals

People who espouse the use of quartz and other stones say that healing energy can be transmitted through and amplified by the molecular structure of natural crystals. This approach to healing is a personal decision, and an area where it is easy to impose your preferences on someone else. Are there currently crystals in the home? Does your friend or family member use crystals as part of their spiritual path? If so, it would be appropriate to place them in your friend's reach or line of vision.

Aromatherapy

Smells can take on a different texture to those who are dying. What was pleasant during good health may be irritating during a transition. So be very careful about burning incense or fragrant candles. Essential oils may also be an irritant to those in their last days. Did the person rely on these aromas during life? If not, then maybe this is not a value-added idea for them now. However if the person specifically requested frankincense, for example, use it sparingly and gauge facial expressions to see if it is becomes too strong.

Water

Our bodies are at least 85% water. As rivers and tributaries bring life to many regions of our planet, so does the path of water in our bodies. From carrying nutrients to where they are needed, transporting oxygen to support our cells, and easing the waste products out of our body, water is a critical part of our health system. With that significance in mind, consider how water has been used in ceremonies throughout history in many civilizations. Here are a few:

- In Africa, water is perceived as a living substance that can help to alleviate misfortunes and the problems of human life.
- For generations, the Hindus have bathed in the Ganges River for purification.

- Buddhists use water in their ceremonies to encourage good fortune in future lives.
- Mayans have been known to hold rituals in cenotes—areas of underground water that collects in sinkholes.
- Native Americans build sweat lodges to purify the mind and body.
- Incan priests were known to sit in stone seats built along water channels to merge their energy with spirit.
- Druids and Wiccans used natural wells for their holy ceremonies and these can still be found today throughout the British Isles.
- Muslims ritually clean their feet and hands with pure water before entering the mosque for prayer.
- Christians use water in Baptism and have other ceremonial functions for Holy Water.
- The Mesopotamian civilizations built a *bitrimki* (washing house) next to the temple and performed a ritual cleansing during the new moon.
- Similar to the Native American sweat lodge, the Aztecs built a *temezcal* using branches and herbs for purification.

Reflecting on some of these practices, you may want to incorporate water into a sacred space. This can be done in a number of ways, both passive and active. Here are some ideas for your consideration.

Passive:

- Place a tabletop water feature in the room to add the soothing sounds of water falling.

- Have a bowl of water in the room with floating flowers or candles. Provide a blessing to the water as a symbol of the life force that continues even after physical death.
- Use a humidifier that has herb or citrus fragrance added to the tank for a fresh feel in the room. (Just be sensitive to any smell that might be overwhelming.)

Active:

- Toast the dying. In a circle (if there are many people) or as a single participant, share a happy memory and raise your glass to honor the life of the person.
- Bathe the feet and hands of the dying with warm water and a gentle cloth. Wipe the face, neck, and shoulders with a loving caress. It can be very unsettling to be without the comfort of a hot shower one used to enjoy.
- Create a soul circle. Each person can hold a small glass of warm water and empty it into a bowl as they make a statement of gratitude. You could then use that water for cleansing as a symbol of a single caring act.

As with all activity in the sacred space, make it special. Make it an act of love and give it the respect that your cherished one deserves.

Music

Music can be the main event in your space or a background to conversation. Depending on your selection it can be a remembrance of a certain life event, for example, some top-40 hits from their high school years. It could represent a period of time like the Big Band era, or even a theme such as Broadway musical hits. I have been in rooms where Frank Sinatra was played for hours because that was the favorite artist of the mother. In this phase of reviewing life and sharing memories these compositions may be appropriate. However the type of music should change over time from songs to instrumental pieces so the dying focus on their journey rather than the lyrics. One of my early home patients had a collection of Mitch Miller, vintage Elvis, and Big band music. I searched for something soothing to play at the end of life and the best I could find was a CD of religious anthems. It occurred to me that the words of these hymns might be the last conscious spiritual instruction he would receive. So of course that would direct him at the time of his transition. There are some great commercially produced sound tracks available, but if you don't have any meaningful meditations or affirmations to play, then I suggest you play soft music only and recite those affirming comments yourself.

Room Temperature

Remember that when one is dying, their body temperature will change. They may feel cool while we in the room are quite warm. Adjust room temperature accordingly and supplement by layering light blankets on the dying person. Avoid anything very thick for two reasons. First, skin can become very fragile in this stage of life and may even become irritated with heavy covers. Second, it can become very confining to have a weighty blanket or comforter covering you when you cannot move very easily.

Visitors

It doesn't matter if you are standing or sitting as long as you are respectful. Sitting would be preferred as it is easier on the patient's neck if they are still able to see. They should not have to strain to maintain eye contact.

Yes, I understand that people don't know what to say, but I cannot emphasize enough that just because a person appears to be unconscious, THEY CAN STILL HEAR YOU!!

I had a coworker who was in her mid-twenties. Lee had a closed-head injury, more commonly known as a stroke. Fortunately she made a recovery, but what she told me about her experience has stuck in my memory for many years. Following the injury and during the first few days of her hospitalization, the doctor would talk to her parents in her room during his rounds. Assuming that because she was in a coma, she would not be able to hear anything, they talked freely about her condition. I was shocked when she relayed the conversation to me. The doctor was telling her parents that it was unlikely that she would come out of the coma. If she did there would be little chance of a normal life for her. Naturally her parents were devastated with this news and were openly grieving her short life.

With her head on a pillow and her body lying lifeless on the vinyl hospital mattress, Lee could hear every word and was incredibly frustrated that she could not communicate. "I'm here. I can hear you," Lee would say inside her head over and over again. As the days continued, that same doctor would come in to her room each morning with his clipboard and pinch her cheek. "Lee? Can you feel that? Does that hurt?" He attempted to provoke a response from her. And she told me she felt it every time and inside her head she was screaming, "You damn right that hurts! Stop it!" As I said, eventually she woke from the coma and today is married with several children, thankfully living a full and healthy life.

A man was visiting his mother as she was beginning to transition under hospice care. The nurse indicated that she had taken the mother's false teeth out and set them in a container on the dresser. He said to the nurse, "I'm glad you told me. I'll take them now so I have them for Field's Funeral home. We need to make sure they are handy when they lay her out." Making comments that refer to a funeral home, burial, or memorial service while a person is dying might re-direct their thoughts from a peaceful and spiritual transition to a physical event that could arouse fear.

Encouragements

Transitional encouraging statements can be soft and relaxing, and they are designed to clear the dying person's mind of any last-held feelings of responsibility. They can be used as a guided imagery technique to allow the person release and comfort.

You are with us through the year.
You are as unique as the snowflake that falls silently on a winter morning.
You are the kindness and generosity of a heart that has loved deeply.
You are the gentle breeze that carries a colorful kite across the meadow.
You are the clean and pure afternoon raindrop that feeds the earth's children.
You are the prettiest flower in the garden, bringing color to our world.
You are the radiance of the first summer sun that warms us.

You are the brightest star in the hot night sky.

You are the frothy wave that crashes against the sandy beach.

You are the sound of children laughing on the first day of school.

You are the sweet and tangy fragrance of an apple orchard at harvest.

You are the serenity of quiet, thankful prayers around the family table.

You are the soft glow of a candle that lights a single window on a cold, dark night.

You are the comfort of a happy ending in the last chapter of a good book.

And you are the thrill of starting a new story that has all the promise of an exciting adventure, because the end of one journey is always the beginning of the next.

Affirmations

Supportive affirmations can be recorded and played softly in the background. There is a corresponding CD set to this book entitled <u>Destination: Higher Self</u>. It can be found through Monroe Products. This set includes affirmations and visualizations that can assist the dying person with their spiritual goals.

I have used these recordings as I provided companionship to the dying. I have seen tense muscles relax and furrowed brows release. Eddie was still communicating when I played *Waves of Light*. As he began to quietly moan with contentment, his eyes started to flutter slightly and when the vocals were complete he said, "Stars. I see millions of stars in a clear black sky. It's beautiful."

Physical Comfort

I expect to have pink sheets with at least a 600-thread count. I want to get into a bed that feels like I'm climbing into a tub of Cool Whip. No scratchy white hospital sheets for me. If I waited to make that desire known at the time of my active dying, chances are I would not have the comfort that I crave. Hospital beds are notoriously uncomfortable. I have heard from several men who were on the plus side of six feet tall that their feet are constantly scrunched up to the footboard or even placed on top of it because their body at rest is longer than the bed. Think about how to make the bedding more comfortable: linens, bed position, overhead lighting, and mood are things we can define now.

If your loved one has not made their final wishes known or it is a sudden event, you may not be sure about how they would like to live through the last days and weeks of their life. Should that be the case, look around the home. Think about how they lived their life. Were they meticulously organized? If so, their room should be the same. For any area, think no clutter, no chaos that would disrupt their ability to process their life's work. Keep it clean and fresh.

If they are still alert and aware, consider their line of vision. Get in the bed yourself and look around. What do you see? Do you see favorite objects and beautiful artwork or a coat rack and a recycling bin? Is the room light at the right height or is it blinding you with a glare from the bulb? Can you talk to visitors without straining your neck?

Many people bring soft, cuddly stuffed animals for their loved one to hold while they are in bed. I have seen this provide some level of comfort, almost as a security article. I do believe that it can partially alleviate the fear of being alone at the end.

The Opportunity of Silence

Silence is an opportunity to examine one's life experience—the ultimate meditation. It is not necessary to keep a TV broadcast or talk radio on to provide artificial company. Our quiet presence is sometimes the most valuable gift we can give. Gently stroking their arm or moving hair away from their eyes is a calm way to show that you are there without being too overwhelming.

If there are things to be said, however, don't pass up this chance to end your physical relationship on a positive note. When the dying person has lost the ability to communicate verbally, we can continue the assistance in other ways. I have said this several times in this book—assume that they can hear every word you say. So perhaps the conversation will be one-way, but it continues to be viable after speech has faded. This is the time for reassurance. It is never too late to say the words you could not say face to face. If you are sorry for something, say so. If you want to forgive your loved one for something in the past, tell them. For some, their generation or cultural background makes saying 'I love you' while maintaining eye contact very difficult. Say it now. Be specific if you can. This might just be what is holding the soul back from making that last step into the next world.

Crying, sobbing or lamenting in a disruptive way will interfere with the soul who is trying to separate. These strong emotions will hold the spirit close to this earthly plane, so asking someone to wait in another area until they regain control would be appropriate. Encourage them to support the dying process rather than create an atmosphere of misery that can bind the soul to the body.

Closing the Space and Releasing the Spirit

So many times when a person dies, the first call is to the funeral home and everyone stands around looking at their shoes waiting for the body to be removed from the area. A closing ceremony can be beneficial for both the recently transitioned and the supporting participants. It directs the soul to move on to the next level and it provides a structured opportunity for goodbyes. Some people are more comfortable with a group ceremony than an individual farewell. If it is possible, do this before the body is moved. With close friends and family participating, this can be a very intimate and memorable gathering.

First, create a healing circle around the bed. Have each person hold a light. This should be a candle if you can do it safely. If not, then use some kind of battery-operated, hand-held lighting.

All: "Ben, we are grateful to have been a part of your time here on Earth. We surround you with love as you move along to the next part of your spiritual journey."

Each individual will then share a grateful moment or loving thought and ask for Ben's soul to move to his higher self. (For example: "Ben you were a great brother. I always felt safe when I was with you and I loved that you were so protective. I wish for you to joyfully move to your higher self now.") As each person is finished speaking, they will extinguish their light and turn to the next person. When all have finished, recite the group chant again.

All: "Ben, we are grateful to have been a part of your time here on Earth. We surround you with love as you move along to the next part of your spiritual journey."

Play affirmations that direct the soul to seek their higher self, soothing music, or both. When you feel that you have finished the ceremony, you can dismantle the area. You might consider using some of the meaningful objects as part of the memorial service or funeral that is held at a later time.

This ritual can also be used if the body is not available or the person died several days, weeks, or even years earlier, should the family think that some closure is needed. Use a photo or profound article in place of the body. This could also release a spirit who has lost their way to the light and needs some encouragement from earthbound friends and family.

During the transition, we should honor the time and space as sacred. You wouldn't talk or take a phone call during someone's wedding or graduation speech. Why should this moment be any less special? This is very likely the most important time in someone's life. They are sometimes struggling between worlds. We owe them a peaceful, quiet atmosphere filled with support and encouragement. I doubt that the dying care if our alarm clock didn't go off this morning, or that the squirrels are eating all of the bird food. Gentle words of encouragement, nature sounds with music, comfortable bedding, and soft lighting can ease someone's physical *and* emotional condition.

CHAPTER 7

The Unexpected Death

"Sometimes the direct path is not the easiest one."

UNKNOWN

IT IS PARTICULARLY upsetting when we lose someone to a sudden death, whether it is a tragic accident, a catastrophic illness such as heart attack or stroke, or even a suicide. However, it is not too late to assist a person in their transition, even if you are not there at the moment of their last breath. Chances are that the soul is so shocked by the event that they would welcome the help of a caring individual, known or not.

Suicide

When someone takes their own life, it can be devastating to those left behind. You might feel guilty—even responsible—and wonder what you could have done to stop it. Or perhaps you are angry, blaming others who should have been able to prevent it. Certainly if that person was close to you, there could be a feeling of abandonment and sadness at how alone you now are. There is some social stigma associated with suicide, so you might be ashamed that your loved could have committed this act, feeling that somehow it reflects a failure on your part. You might be hesitant to talk about it with anyone. And your friends may not know what to say, so they don't say anything or tread so gently around you that it is uncomfortable for you both. Grief is hard anyway, and suicide brings with it another whole set of circumstances for you to deal with.

If this should happen to someone who is close to you, it is not too late to aid their transition. You might have to temporarily put some of your low frequency emotional reactions on hold in order to support this soul. Just because a person ends their own life doesn't mean that they are not deserving of all the assistance we can give to their nonphysical evolution. From a spiritual perspective, we cannot judge the path of another; but we can help to provide some direction for them to achieve a more conscious death.

Suicide Prayer

This is an example of how you could send healing energy to someone who has taken their own life. To make it more personal, specific details about their life could be added. The important thing to convey is that you wish them well and that you respect the path they have taken. You may not like it or agree with it; and as difficult as it might be to set your emotional or logical response aside for the moment, if you are in a position to assist in a tragic transition—why would you hesitate?

Prayer for a Suicide
"Our Dearest Sally,
We love you, we support you. We send light to your spirit.
If you seek forgiveness, it is given without hesitation.

If you are lost, we pray that you look to the direction that will take you home and that your travels will fulfill you.
If you are in pain, we pray that cooling relief fills your spirit, providing comfort and healing.
If you are sad, we pray that pure joy saturates your heart and that you will find bliss wherever you go.
If you are lonely, we pray that you will find and embrace those souls who are meant to wrap you in love and friendship.
If you miss us as we miss you, know that we will be together again if it is meant to be.
We are heartbroken at this loss, but we support your path. For all that you have been to us—we thank you for being such a meaningful part of our lives here on Earth.
We honor your journey now and always."

Losing a Child

When someone loses a baby through either a miscarriage, a still birth, disease, or an accident, it is a loss just as painful as any other. Some think it is worse. You have lost not only a baby, but also all the experiences that would follow. There are no first steps, no first teeth or first words. You lose the excitement of the first day of school, the first prom date, and potentially a wedding. The mother and father will never know the person their baby would have become. This is a loss that is felt over and over again. If you have not had this experience, then it is difficult to even conceive of the pain that parents must feel.

With the loss of a child, the sequence of events disturbs what we perceive as the natural order of things. Parents are older and should die first. Having a memorial for your child must be overwhelming for the entire family. Few words would be sufficient to ease the pain. If the parents are unable to perform any kind of ceremony, this is a time to ask for assistance from a close friend or family member. Below is a sample prayer that could be modified to fit the specific family situation.

Prayer for a Child

Our precious child,
In all the families around the world, we thank you for choosing us.
We are honored that you were here in our lives. Even though we
have known you for just a short time, we appreciate the gifts you
have given us. During these treasured moments we learned how
to love with all of our hearts. We learned about being thankful
for every minute you spent with us, and most of all we now know
that life needs to be cherished and we should make each day count.
We are relieved that you are no longer in pain. We know you are
surrounded in love and peace and that has brought some comfort
to us. We will always carry you in our hearts, but we are grateful
that you have returned to God and your spiritual home.

It can be difficult to console a grieving parent, but sidestepping the truth is even worse. Parents do not want to forget their lost child, so changing the subject or avoiding a conversation altogether is not supportive. It may be comforting to hear a memory about their baby. "I always will remember her first birthday and how she dove into that cake. She was so funny with that pink icing all over her face." You could mention something that was physically endearing such as "her deep brown eyes" or "such a comical little laugh." End the comments with something like,

"We will all miss her very much. I feel lucky to have known her, even for such a short time. I am so sorry that we lost her. Is there anything that I can do to help you now or later down the road?"

Ending Life Support

Life-support techniques are medical interventions that will keep a person's body 'alive' without hope of recovery. These include but are not limited to ventilation tubing to assist breathing, feeding tubes to provide nutrition, and IV lines that provide a variety of assistance including antibiotics. Some would also classify dialysis and chemotherapy as prolonging a life that will eventually succumb to the disease that the procedures are treating. You should confer with your medical team to get more information about these options.

When someone has been declared to be in a persistent vegetative state (brain dead) by two attending physicians, then there is said to be no hope for recovery. The body has completely lost its ability to function independently. Sometimes we will extend the physical life due to a selfish desire to keep our loved one with us. Maybe you are hoping for a miracle that is not going to come (based on the logical information that has been provided to you). They, as you knew them, are already gone and that fact can be tough to rationalize during an emotional time. If you accept the truth that the soul is separate and has only used the physical body for transportation, it will make much more sense to let their spirit soar. Create a picture in your mind where you are opening a box and releasing a dove. You are allowing her to fly high and far to a freedom that is not possible on this earth. Once understood, then you should be in the position to release the soul who is trapped in a nonfunctioning physical body.

This is an honor, albeit sometimes a sad one, and should be accompanied by a sacred moment in time. Just because someone is dying in a medical facility doesn't mean that we can't provide them with all the spiritual support one could give at home. Here is an example of affirmations for someone on life support who is about to have their spirit released. Ask for quiet and privacy from the staff. Repeat the following affirmations. The timing should be based on your intuitive judgement. Say it with love, knowing the truth of our existence.

Affirmations at the End of Life
You are safe, returning to the source.
You are flowing in the path of light.
You embrace the flow of your spiritual essence.
You are on your way home.
You have unlimited energy to follow your spiritual path.
You are easily moving along the journey to spiritual enlightenment.
You joyfully go to the clear light of your source.
You are surrounded by love moving along your spiritual path.
You separate from the physical to consciously become your higher self.

Refer to Chapter 6: *Creating a Sacred Space and Time* for some additional ideas about closing ceremonies. You might want to combine prayers, affirmations, and closing ceremony words from other parts of this book.

In the end, remember that it is the disease or medical condition that has ended the life of your loved one—not the person who makes the decision regarding the time to discontinue the artificial accessories. If it makes you more comfortable, you can always confer with the facility chaplain, social worker, or other concerned loved ones.

Tragic Accidents

When Bill and I were talking about the impact of an accident or disaster, he told me a story about one of his many cross-country flights.

I was on a commercial flight on my way to Portland, Oregon. It had been mostly uneventful until the pilot came out of the cockpit and walked down the center of the plane. He asked a few people who were seated by the wing to step out into the aisle for a moment. This was directly in front of me. As their seats were emptied he leaned into the row and looked out at the wing. I could see some subtle streams of smoke coming from underneath. This can't be good, I thought.

The pilot went back into the cockpit and made the following announcement. "Good afternoon. This is the captain speaking. I'd like to have your attention for a minute. We have a situation with one of the engines. Now we don't think it's serious, but we are going to make an unscheduled landing in Kansas City just to have it checked out." Immediately the flight attendants put away the beverage service and began to check our seatbelts. We were then told that there was a potential for an emergency landing so we were instructed on the correct posture for a rough arrival (aka: crash). Bend over and place your hands over your head.

By this time, the other passengers were praying, crying, grabbing each other's hands, and generally beginning to panic. I closed my eyes and began an affirmation in my mind. "Now I go to my higher self." I repeated this in my mind with no fear, knowing that if the plane did indeed crash, I would be in the right mindset to achieve my goal of reaching my higher self.

As we circled, dumping fuel, I could begin to see all of the emergency equipment on the runway waiting for our plane to land. I felt fortunate to have these few moments of awareness to recite my mantra, "Now I go to my higher self."

As you may have guessed, the plane landed softly without incident, but I had a renewed sense of confidence that should I be in a life-threatening emergency again in the future, I will be prepared to direct my consciousness to my higher self.

WILLIAM

Even if you are not present for an end-of-life moment, there are still opportunities for you to support someone's transition. Repeating verbal or silent affirmations, providing guidance to experience their higher self or sending light and love to assist their journey can be helpful. Today many repeat their guidance for several days and even weeks after death.

CHAPTER 8

※

Release the Spirit

"One is never afraid of the unknown; one is afraid of the known coming to an end."

JIDDU KRISHNAMURIT

The Impact of Grief

ONCE THE PHYSICAL death has occurred and the support provided by friends and family has dwindled, one will most likely continue to experience some level of grief. Grief is not a disease; it is a natural and normal reaction to loss. We have all experienced it at different levels through various events in our lives. Grief can show up during the end of a rewarding career, a marriage, or the loss of a home. It should not be rushed; everyone grieves on their own schedule. There are multiple stages defined by researchers and educators, but all you know is that you feel terrible and you wonder if it is ever going to stop. Why do we feel so sad when we lose someone close to us?

You might feel afraid of the new responsibilities that you have inherited. If you know nothing about the home finances because your wife always took care of the checkbook, then you have to learn this new process right in the middle of mourning your loss. Emotionally you could feel abandoned by a person who had pledged to be by your side for the long term and now they are gone— possibly without warning. You turn to tell them a funny story from your trip to the grocery store and no one is there to hear it. The vacation trip of a lifetime will never be. There could be unresolved issues; an apology that you had been working on cannot be offered or an introduction that had been waiting for the right moment will never happen. Your life may never be the same, but perhaps it is exactly how it should be.

A Spiritual Approach to Grief

We can take a different approach to grief to help us move beyond the initial emotional reaction and into the true essence of what we are and why we are here.

Acknowledge the spiritual truth. We are spiritual beings having a human experience. Our body is merely a tool to move us around this earth in order for us to complete our human education. They are convenient trappings that we are using to gain experience and learn about Earth life's challenges. From before we are born, we know that we are here for only a finite amount of time. Maybe it is 97 minutes, maybe it is 97 years— but we know when we come here that we will someday dispose of the physical body that no longer serves us. Although we have some control or forethought about our own end, we cannot control or predict the death of another.

Understand the purpose of your connection. With as much objectivity as you can muster, create a theory of why the two of you were placed together. Perhaps you lost a child who was just ten years old. Did your son teach you to look through the eyes of a child to love simply and honestly? Maybe you have gained a better appreciation for life by seeing one end at such a young age. It could be a chance to show unconditional love and patience while caring for someone who was very ill. There are no wrong answers. Whatever you decide is absolutely true. And it is OK to re-evaluate at a later time when you have even more life experience to use for reference.

Honor the job well done. Once you understand the purpose of your relationship, then you can celebrate the accomplishment. After identifying the connection with your spouse, you see that he was partnered with you to help resolve your fears. With him, you felt free to venture out into the world and have new experiences. You took risks and had adventures with him that you never would have had alone. Thank him for that gift and schedule a trip to a UNESCO site in his honor. Show him that he was successful and you have developed into a courageous human being. As time moves along, you might find yourself challenged by something significant and reflecting on your relationship may give you the resolution you need to emerge victorious.

Identify and accomplish your spiritual mission. After recognizing the connection and honoring the intention of it, take some time to focus on your own spiritual purpose. Your younger sister lived with you for many years as she tried to overcome her battle with depression. You believe your connection was to support her while she tried to put her life in order. After years of treatment, she took her own life and now you question your real purpose. So you study the disease relentlessly and volunteer in a local mental health clinic. You search for answers about this illness until you become an expert and over time you find yourself helping dozens of people address issues in their family. Several of your success stories are written and published in the community paper, you set up a non-profit organization that raises money for treatment, and you become an important part of battling this disease. It hits you—supporting your sister was a by-product of your real mission. Her sacrifice through suicide has provided you the opportunity to help many other souls overcome their own emotional struggles. Congratulations! You have assisted the evolution of others.

Multiple Examples of Grief in the Same Household

Reflect on this case study based on a question that I received from a concerned family member. You can see examples of several types of grief and how the individuals are harming not only each other but also the soul of the one they lost.

My brother and sister-in-law have lost a child. Why do they fight all the time instead of supporting each other?

I am sorry for their loss. The death of a child is devastating and this must be a very difficult time for them. If they haven't already taken advantage of grief counseling, I would highly recommend it. Everyone grieves differently and that can cause unnecessary tension. Let me use an example of how a family can be in constant conflict over this kind of loss. Let's call the mother Jane and the father Tim.

Since the loss of baby Leo, Jane weeps most of the day. She openly sobs during TV shows and slams the pots and pans when she gets around to cooking dinner. Frequently moaning on the phone with her friends, she wonders how this could have happened to her. She is a good person, after all. Sleeping through the night is just a memory and putting on makeup seems pointless. She has stopped going to the gym and no longer makes sales appointments in her real estate office. Jane is having trouble with everything she does because she can't focus on anything but Leo. She can't understand why Tim doesn't feel the same way.

Tim has returned to work, and although he is also deeply hurt he manages to stay effective in his management job. Because his wife has stopped working, he knows that he must ensure that the family finances stay intact. He also thinks about Leo frequently, but his mourning drives him to become withdrawn and quiet. His friends extend their sympathies but he doesn't want to talk about it. He works late most nights in order to avoid interacting with his shattered wife. When he does come home, he retreats to his den, sitting in silence for hours. His role as family protector has been compromised and seeing the constant tears of his wife is a cruel reminder. He wonders if he will ever stop feeling so sad and inadequate.

They have a teenage son who is watching how his parents deal with their grief. He doesn't know how to feel about the family loss, because no one is talking to him about it. Actually, his parents are barely speaking to him at all, missing school appointments and his baseball games. He turns to his friends for companionship in the evening. To hide his pain, he begins to drive recklessly—even participating in street races after midnight. The thrill makes him feel alive and when the crowd cheers him on, it provides the attention he craves.

You can see how this family is in trouble. Each of them is grieving, but in their own way. No one is sadder than the other, although they would appear to be. They have lost their connection to each other and that makes for a secondary loss. What they aren't considering is that it is very likely that Leo is still with them in spirit, shackled to the lower planes as a result of his family's emotional reaction and resulting behavior.

They must take time to consider each other, and grief counseling is a good way for them to reconnect as a family. Performing a closing ceremony that releases Leo's spirit will give them back some of the power that they have lost. Unity and support for each other is the best way to honor the memory of Leo.

Journaling

Journaling can be very valuable as you sort through your feelings about a loss. Writing can be an opportunity for creativity as well as a safe place to reflect. Select a book that will bring honor to your entries. Make it special, with a luxurious cover, pages that welcome your words, and a comfortable binding that makes it a pleasure to open. Keep it in a convenient place where is easy to find and replace, yet private enough to keep curious eyes away.

- Write about your grief, how it makes you feel.
- Write a message to your loved one expressing gratitude for their part in your life.
- Write the things you wished you had said but never did.
- Write supportive comments for your loved one as they return home.
- Write about your dreams. (They may be different now.)
- Write about your plans for the future.
- Write about the good things that are happening to you in order to keep balance.

Use this process as an outlet for stress or sadness by giving yourself permission to express your emotions. This can be the voice you feel most comfortable using until you can see beyond the pain and regret. Look back to the beginning after you have written for some months. See how your feelings have changed, how far you've come.

If you have a friend who has just lost a family member, perhaps the gift of a special journal and a beautiful pen can be more impactful than a vase of flowers.

Holding onto Grief

Near our home is a small business where the owner sells mulch, stones, and seed. A few years ago, he had a portable sign placed in his parking lot that said, *"My son was killed by an impaired driver. Five years for taking a life. Does that sound fair to you?"* I was sorry that the man had lost a child to violence, and even more so that the killer had been given such a short sentence. It must have been heartbreaking for this family. Recently the sign had been changed to, *"My son has been gone for 3 years. The pain never stops for us."* I was moved to think that now there is a second tragedy. The young man may not be able to move on as long as his father's anger is so intense. If the universe could write to the grieving dad, this is what the letter might say.

Dear Mr. Mulch,

First I would like to say that I am very sorry for your loss. It must be incredibly painful to lose a child and then be given a second gut punch by seeing your son's killer serve an inappropriately short sentence. I am certain that you miss him very much. I hear you pray every day that he could be returned to you so your life could go back to the way it was before he was taken so abruptly. But sadly, that is not how it will work out.

Imagine if you can, your son's spirit hovering around you, crying when you cry, and shouting out in anger when you think you can't take it any longer. See him as frustrated as you are when you reread the legal documents that detail the crime, and watch him bend over in pain as you once again look at his untouched room. You need to see your son as a mirror of your emotional state, because that is what is happening. As long as you hold these intense but unproductive emotions, your son will not be

239

able to move on to his spiritual home. He will continue to live on the lower astral plane because he is tied to your anger. I don't believe you would want your beautiful son to suffer any longer. It is like holding onto the foot of a little bird. He wants to fly, but he is bound to you by your grief.

Thankfully, you have the power to release him anytime. Forgive all who were involved and give him permission, even encouragement, to fly to his highest potential. Send gratitude to him for spending even a short period of time in your life. It was a gift that you will treasure for all time. You will meet again someday and those who were part of the events that led to this moment will have their day in a higher court. Don't let them rob you of the rest of your life too.

Sincerely,

The Universe

Pet Loss

Losing a pet can trigger many of the same emotions that are felt when one loses a human companion; there can be feeling of anger, guilt, depression, and even denial. In many households, a pet is like a family member—providing friendship, loyalty, entertainment, and even protection. So when the pet passes, a hole is left in the family life. This can be even worse if a disease drove a decision to euthanize. The guilt and second guessing can be emotionally consuming.

So if you know someone who has lost a dog or a cat from either illness or accident, show them the same caring attitude that you would if they had suffered the loss of a person who was close to them. In fact, creating a sacred space, using music and affirmations for comfort, or even enlisting the aid of a doula may be appropriate for your friend. Take their memorial services seriously and allow them to grieve without criticism or unwanted advice. A comment such as, "You can get a replacement" is no more welcome than if it was a family member who had passed. There is a website listed in the resource section of this book for more detailed information.

There are no early deaths—each one occurs at the exact right time. However, your grief may tell you something far different. So consider this. You can recognize your loved one as a spiritual being or as a human being. If you focus on the human, then you will yearn for the physical aspects like companionship, conversation, and the social connection you shared. This causes pain that can interfere with your daily activity and even how you interact with others. If you see them as a spiritual being, then you can better appreciate the time they chose to spend with you. Rather than be angry or hurt that you didn't get enough time with them, reflect on the joy that you did have and honor that gift by allowing the soul to move on.

It is important to remember that once the physical body has ceased to function, the soul (or spirit) that inhabited that body may still be present. We can assist that spirit to move on to the dimension that is right for their spiritual development. How we grieve and the type of farewell ceremony we design can have an impact on their ability to move on.

CHAPTER 9

Celebrate the Life Experience

"Goodbyes are for those who love with their eyes, because for those who love with their heart and soul, there is no separation."

RUMI

CELEBRATING THE LIFE of those who have died is not a new idea. Ceremonies and rituals have been performed in various ways throughout history. As far back as the Stone Age, there is evidence of respect for those who have gone before us. Cave drawings suggest that the spirits of ancestors were welcomed and remained present to advise their descendants and pass on visions. Around the world there are hundreds, if not thousands, of cultural rituals surrounding the death of a community member. A Pagan makes nature offerings to honor the dead, a Mormon sees death as a time of hope assisting one into eternal life with God, and a Jewish family sits Shiva for a seven-day mourning period. As humans we honor the dead across geographic and cultural borders.

Home Funeral

"Slowing down the process allows all involved to absorb the loss at their own pace. It's an organic, emotional and spiritual healing not available from limited calling hours at a remote location." This is from Elizabeth Knox, founder of *Crossings*—a home-based funeral service in Maryland, and former member of the Board of Directors of the National Home Funeral Alliance (NHFA).

What is a home funeral? This is a do-it-yourself service where family and friends gather and participate at home (or other sacred space) to say goodbye to a deceased friend or family member. This can include after-death rituals, preparing the body, transporting the body, final disposition of the remains, and even filing for the death certificate. A professional funeral director may participate in some partial capacity, or not at all. State regulations vary, so be sure to check on the laws in your area.

The NHFA provides educational resources and advocates for the rights of families. If you think this might be a good option for you, I have listed their web site in the reference section of this book.

Planning a Memorial Service

Timing and location - Traditional memorial services through funeral homes occur very quickly, within days or even hours of the viewing and visitation. That is not a requirement. If there is a special time of year, a memorial service honoring a life can be held months later. With our friends and families scattered across the country and sometimes the world, it might be very appropriate to have a ceremony when all can attend.

Funeral homes and churches are typical locations for a farewell, but for many of us it can be impersonal and even contradictory to how we have lived our lives. Be creative and choose a place that would be meaningful such as a beach, park, forest, or farm. Natural settings are a great selection, but if an institution like a school, museum, or non-profit organization was very important, then find a meeting area on the grounds that would be appropriate for your group and agenda.

Participants/Invitees - If you are planning a ceremony that is outside of the traditional religious ritual or funeral home, you should consider how you will notify people about the event. In these days of social media, there are a variety of options. Just be aware of the reach of the invitation if you need to limit the number of people who attend. If you are unsure, revert to what the departed would want. If they were very social, with memberships in many organizations, then make the memorial a community event. A quiet homebody would appreciate a more private ceremony.

Don't feel like you have to plan the whole thing yourself. If you are grieving, there is enough on your plate. All those friends who have been asking what they could do to help would be more than happy to pitch in and check on chair rentals, create custom music collections, or set up parking arrangements. There are also professional event planners that can assist.

Music and atmosphere - There is a great selection of music to consider. If religious music is not on the playlist for your loved one, then take a look at favorite groups, styles, or time periods. The mood can be set as celebratory with music that is complementary to a life well lived. Providing printed lyrics could encourage a sing-along from the participants.

Words and verse- People who have been significant in the life of the honoree could be asked to speak. This can be an individually written description of their relationship with some anecdotes and personal thoughts. There are also many available readings that might be appropriate for the event. You could provide handouts with a favorite poem or passage from a meaningful book. If the deceased was not a religious person, then I would suggest that you not use scripture or words from other holy texts as this would not be consistent with the person's life.

Ceremony Ideas

Here are some thought-starters to honor your departed loved one in a nontraditional way.

Bouquet of Life – Ask each participant to bring a single-stemmed flower that best reminds them of the deceased. At the front of the space, have an empty vase. During the ceremony, ask each person to place their flower in the vase. As an option, you could have them say a single word or phrase that describes the person as they place their stem into the container. At the end there will be a beautiful bouquet that represents the heart and soul of the loved one.

Modifications: This can also be modified to be a sand or stone collection. Ask each person to select a stone and write a single word that describes the person. Once placed into a glass container this becomes a stone 'garden' that can be repositioned to a memorial site at a later time. Another variation is the emptying of a sand vial to an empty glass container. This can represent the notion that we are all part of a collective consciousness.

Life Light – At the beginning of the service, have someone light a single candle at the front of the space. This candle will represent the deceased. At some point, have each person take a tapered candle from a stack and light their candle from the main flame. This can be a representation of how the deceased has provided light to the participants. After a release prayer, extinguish all the candles but encourage participants to keep them as an occasional remembrance in the days to come.

Love Notes – Provide a box, small note papers, and pencils to the participants. Invite each person to write a word, a memory, or a thought of thanks to the departed. When all of the notes have been placed in the box, the leader can say a few words to thank and release the spirit. At that point, the contents of the box could be burned, shredded, or buried.

Life Celebration Board – In a designated space, install a poster board either on an easel or attached to the wall. On a table nearby, have a selection of markers in various colors. (The color selection could reflect the love of a sports team, scholastic location or just an assorted grouping.) Ask each guest to write something that they learned from the person who has died. At first, people may be shy so ask a few people to start the board; eventually there will be many notes for all to read. This helps to refresh memories and pass along the many lessons people have gathered from the honoree.

Honoring without Obsessing

Consider this excerpt from Chapter 18 of <u>Adventures in the Afterlife</u>. It is a story about attachment and grieving that could apply to many people.

In the distance I see a middle-aged woman standing on the bank of a river and she appears to be calling out the name of her daughter. On the opposite river bank a girl of about twelve years old looks panic-stricken as tears stream down her cheeks. The girl strains to hear the voice of her mother from across the river and repeatedly calls out her mother's name and then waits for a response. All I can hear are faint, mumbled words that sound like prayers echoing across the water. I can clearly feel the deep desperation and loneliness of the girl as my guide speaks.

"This girl died several months ago and remains strongly attached to her Earth mother. The mother's yearning to have her back in her physical life is hampering the girl's ability to progress with her spiritual evolution. She refuses to let her go and calls out to her daughter with repeated prayers. This soul is hindered by her mother's extreme attachment because she continues to project thoughts of loss and grief instead of love. How can any soul move onward when they are held by the powerful hooks of thought?"

"Why doesn't someone help to guide the girl to a higher reality?"

"Several have tried, including her grandmother, but she continues to hear her mother's pleading thoughts and refuses to move on. She fears she will lose her mother forever if she moves out of thought range. Prolonged grieving and attachment over the dead can become an act of self-pity. The mother would serve her daughter best by sending prayers releasing her from the past physical life and all her attachments to Earth. She could pray for the light of God's love to surround and protect their daughter from all influences that might block her spiritual progress. Any prayer or intention focused on unconditional love and spiritual release would be helpful."

The Hindus believe that prolonged grieving can hold the soul in earthly consciousness, inhibiting their full transition. Because the departed soul is very aware of emotional focus directed at him, Hindus encourage joyous release instead of long periods of mourning. You can honor your loved one without blocking their spiritual progress.

There is a saying that funerals are for the living. I actually see two beneficiaries in a ceremony honoring a life that has ended. The first is to provide a ritual that that allows the living to say goodbye. It should include sights and sounds that celebrate the life and mission of the deceased. It is a forum for those who have had meaningful relationships to honor that relationship and say goodbye.

The second is to release the soul who may still be lingering. With words and actions, in our role as physical beings, we can demonstrate to those who have passed that the time has come for them to move on. Think of helping your loved one onto a bus that will take them to the destination of their desire. It is very possible that they will need your encouragement to take these last few steps. This can be done minutes, days, or even years after the physical death, but the sooner we communicate the easier it is for their spirit to move on.

Funerals, memorial services, and wakes are all very personal events. They should reflect the character and significant moments in the life of the deceased. This can be done based on personal knowledge, a written plan, or by chance with a stranger at the helm. The good news is that you have a choice right now, at this moment, on how it will be. Documenting is the key to making it happen.

CHAPTER 10

Document your Spiritual Directive

"The bitterest tears shed over graves are for words left unsaid and deeds left undone."

HARRIET BEECHER STOWE

YOU SPEND MONTHS planning your vacation. You know when you will leave, where you will stay, and what attractions you will schedule into each day. After all, it is your big week and you want everything to turn out just right. When you buy a car, there are websites to investigate and anecdotal information to gather from your friends and neighbors. The dealer ratings and locations are posted for your review. You will most likely use all of these resources to make your selection. So when it comes to your transition from this world into the next, why would you leave all of these details to another person—possibly even someone who never knew you as a living, breathing, spiritual being?

Designing your Transition

At this point you have a pretty good idea of the physical and emotional impact of dying a gradual death. Decisions about using hospice services and doulas can be made more easily with

249

the information that has been presented. You know how to assist someone who has had a sudden, tragic death. Those who need to be forgiven have been and you have expressed gratitude to the people in your life who deserve it. You know what to say to someone who is dying and you have some ideas about addressing issues of grief. Planning your memorial service seems more achievable and you are ready to put your plan to paper.

I had a Reiki session with Marianne, a lady in her early 70s. We met in her daughter's apartment where the hospital bed took up most of the floor space in her small living room. She was actively dying and non-communicative. Marianne was very organized and had made her funeral arrangements the week she found out that her illness was terminal. She had her dress picked out and had selected the casket in which she would wear it. Her obituary was written, her church had been notified, and the cemetery was on standby. The daughter commented on how she had planned everything in advance so that her children would not have to do it. I admire this lady, as she did not shy away from what would have been easy to leave for someone else. Regardless of what her spiritual convictions were, she certainly set the stage for her own fearless transition.

Now is the time to surround yourself with good people. Develop a team of kindred spirits so that when the time comes they are ready to spring into action to make sure that your plan is carried out without hesitation.

The Spiritual Directive

In the appendix of this book, you will find a Spiritual Directive Worksheet. There are designations for everything from naming a doula to choosing a color scheme. There are spaces for messages as well as an area to list physical conditions that you consider important. It is divided into three distinct sections.

Section 1: While I am dying – *If I can no longer communicate for myself.*
This is directed toward the sacred space area and allows for identification of meditations, music, and other items for someone to provide for you.
Section 2: Unfinished Business – *People to contact, messages to give should I die suddenly.*
In the event that you are unable to have those forgiveness and gratitude discussions, this allows you to identify who needs to hear from you and what you would like to say.
Section 3: Memorial Wishes – *When the time comes to say goodbye.*
Here is the place where you can specify the kind of memorial service that would be most meaningful to you. Anything from music, location, and readings can be listed. There is also a space for you to distinguish what you do not want. Your parting words to the attendees can be written here as well.

Take some time to complete this document. It will give you a chance to see if you have any gaps in your planning. Once completed, meet with a trusted friend or relative to discuss your wishes. Ideally, a few of you can do this together. Be sure to select someone who has the authority to make these desires known and completed. It would be very frustrating to go through this analysis only to have your sibling decide on something completely different. Check with your own legal expert to verify the enforcement of this document; however, generally a signature with a Notary Public witness is sufficient.

Community Groups

The objective of a Death Café is "to increase awareness of death with a view to helping people make the most of their (finite) lives." This quote is from their web site www.deathcafe.com. There is no agenda, no objectives or themes in these informal meetings, just a group of acquaintances who meet for coffee and talk about death. This phenomenon began in 2010 under the direction of Jon Underwood in the United Kingdom, based on the work of Bernard Crettay. There is a presence on Facebook and Twitter as well as a guide to starting your own group on their website.

In the Cincinnati area of the U.S., there is a group called Coffee and Caskets that conducts end-of-life discussions over a hot beverage and snack. They have many interesting posts on Pinterest. With a little research, I am sure you can find something in your area or even start your own.

And Then There's the Practical Stuff . . .

In order to focus fully on our spiritual evolution during our last days, it helps to have some of the practical information accounted for. There are so many legal documents, asset distribution opportunities, contacts, and website passwords that it will take a detailed map to direct your beneficiaries to all the information that they need to settle your estate. If you are worried about the disposition of your assets and physical belongings, it will be difficult to direct your attention to becoming connected to your higher self.

Where is your information stored? – Select a safe place that is fire and water proof. This could be a locked box in your home or at your bank. It could be kept in the office of the attorney who will serve as your executor. The important thing is that the affected people know where it is. You can't assume that they will be able to find everything unless you identify the location prior to your passing.

Contact Information – A document should be easily accessible that has your personal information such as your full name, birthplace, and social security number. Your phone number(s), address, and e-mail account(s) should be listed. This document should include not only the specifics of you and/or your partner but also those of anyone who needs to be notified. Are there people whom you would like to have called immediately? What about any organizations that you belong to? Is your calendar handy so any upcoming obligations are clearly identified?

Legal Documents – This includes insurance, asset distribution, vital records, as well as wills, trusts and advanced directives. If you have any pre-arrangement requests that have been documented, are they quickly available? Timing can be a factor in determining whether your desires are fulfilled.

Advanced Directive Forms Website – There is a website that will lead you to the legal forms that you can use when outlining your medical needs at the end of life. It is www.caringinfo.org. These are listed by state so that you can choose the forms that are appropriate for you (U.S. residents). This will address life support and resuscitation decisions. Please consult your legal professional when making and documenting these choices.

Almost Last Words

Those of us who have seen someone die know that it is unlikely that they will say something profound and then fall back into their pillow with a sigh as they take the last breath. But there are some very insightful comments spoken as people are nearing their end. I have captured a few here that I have personally heard. I invite you to look at these and begin to imagine what your last words might be.

"Spend your money now on the things you want to see and do, otherwise you will end up like me—giving it all away to strangers."

"I never thought it would end like this. I don't have my house in order. My kids will have to deal with it."

"I just can't do the things I used to do without a lot of pain. Simple things like loading the dishwasher. I just can't do it anymore and that's what is depressing." (Have you complained about the kitchen chores lately?)

"Who would have thought that even at this stage in my life I could learn something new?" (This was said to me by a patient after she had her first Reiki treatment.)

"I've had a pretty decent life. I know it's my time. I'm ready to go."

"I thought I'd come back. There was another day on the calendar, so I thought I'd use it."

"I ask God if when I get to heaven I could take of the animals. I love animals, all kinds. Do you think he'll let me do that?"

"I'm looking for my car keys. Do you know where they are? I'd like to take a drive now."

"I don't even know how old I am anymore, but I guess it doesn't really matter, does it?"

"Everything happens for a reason, good things and bad things. The bad things are a wake up for you."

"I am one of 12 children. They have all died, but I don't think they would want to come back to this world anyway."

"Call the manager. I have some things to say." (Since we were in his home, I took it to mean a higher power not the building administrator.)

"That's enough. Goodnight." (This was spoken by a woman who had already begun actively dying. She mumbled this about 24 hours before she passed.)

"My (deceased) husband came to visit me. I told him he should leave before he couldn't find his way back. He said he could with no problem, but I wasn't sure so I sent him away."

"You know, God has given a purpose to everyone. You might not know what it is, but it's there. You just have to find it."

"People seem to require so many things that they don't really require."

"I've lived long enough. I'm ready for the next group of people I'm supposed to be with."

CLOSING THOUGHTS

> *"As you rise with the morning sun, think of what a pre-*
> *cious privilege it is to be alive,*
> *to breathe, to think, to enjoy, to love."*

MARCUS AURELIUS

In this world we are busy chasing our dreams, acquiring things to make our life more comfortable, and thinking about what we can do to improve our future prospects. We are often obsessed with the latest technology, fascinated by celebrity news, and consumed with achieving career goals. When we are able to trade up in size or style when buying a piece of jewelry, a new car, or a house, it is considered a measure of our success.

With this in mind, I noticed a certain minimalism as I entered one man's room to sit as a doula. They asked me to visit this man in a tone that suggested he wasn't likely to have anyone else come to see him. There were no family photos, greeting cards, or flowers in his room. I noticed on the inventory chart sitting on the dresser that zero personal belongings were brought in. I sat by him with a unique view. Without all the surrounding decoration it was just his weak and broken body.

All of his life and everything he had experienced, every place he had visited, and everyone he had ever known were just distant memories. All he had was the here and now, and not much left of that. The only thing he was carrying with him was his soul. I prayed for him that even though his body was failing and his breath was labored, his spirit would be strong enough to carry him to the next level of his spiritual evolution. I asked that everything that had led up to this moment would guide him to his higher self.

Our soul has no pockets. When we die we carry nothing with us, but we'll take everything that we have done. Will you take your best with you?

Appendix

Spiritual Directive

Planning Document

1. While I am dying: If I can no longer communicate.
My selected doula is:

_____

In my Sacred Space:
The location I would like to be during my last days:

_____

The music I would like to hear:

_____

I consider special objects to be:

_____

I would like to have these mediations/affirmations/essays playing in my last days:

_____

_____

_____

_____

_____

_____

_____

Additional things to consider:

2. Unfinished Business: Messages should I die suddenly.

If I don't have time to say it: _____

_____

_____

_____

Honor my memory by: _____

_____

_____

I am most grateful in my life for: _____

_____

_____

_____

I seek forgiveness from: _____

_____

_____

I forgive: _____

_____

_____

My highest spiritual intention is: _____

_____

_____

_____

3. Memorial Wishes: When the time comes to say goodbye.

My color preferences are: _____

My favorite music selections are: _____

_____

_____

Attached are some readings or quotes that I like:

_____

_____

_____

Thoughts about flowers and charitable contributions:

_____

_____

_____

My ideal memorial service would be: _____

_____

_____

_____

(location, time of day, setting, etc.)

Please <u>do not</u> do this: _____

_____

My words of farewell: _____

_____

_____

Questions and Comments

Part One

What is the purpose of physical existence?

The physical world provides a brilliantly conceived training environment for developing souls; its primary function is the evolution of consciousness through intense personal experience. We are a nonphysical species using temporary biological bodies as vehicles for our developing consciousness. Each soul creates their individualized educational curriculum by the choices they make and the resulting actions they take. The magnificent training system of life is self-sustaining and fully automatic; universal energy laws such as cause and effect mean you experience and learn from what you sow. Our physical life and all the diverse challenges function as a magnificent educational system. The result is extremely effective, for there is no escaping the individual lessons we experience from our own thoughts and deeds. Since we are immortal the length of time our training may take is meaningless; eventually everyone graduates.

Is going to the light sufficient to experience liberation?

No. When we enter any higher-vibrational reality it will appear much brighter and lighter than the physical world. When first entering the astral dimension, it will appear as a brilliant light when compared to the density of matter. Be aware, the pleasant nonphysical realities that most humans experience at death exist far from our true spiritual home. It is essential to be very specific and focused when using our mantras during all altered states of consciousness, OBEs, NDEs and especially at death. Never settle for the mundane physical reflections of Earth. Aim high, Spiritual Liberation Now!

What are the initiations of soul you speak about in your workshops?

Essentially, initiations are personal experiences and challenges that lead to a lasting shift of consciousness in the individual. Initiations can manifest as any form of trial or obstacle that must be overcome in order to experience personal growth. There are two major kinds of initiations. One is an expansion or shift of consciousness within the current dimensional environment of the individual (for example, confronting and resolving a deep-seated personal fear or limitation). The other kind of initiation is a transition of consciousness from one dimension to another and the resulting change from a denser energy body to a higher-frequency energy body within us. An example would be an experience that leads to the expansion of consciousness from the astral body and the full activation and integration into the individual's higher-vibrational mental/thought-energy body.

What is the single most common issue that hinders our spiritual progress in the afterlife?

After death our continuing attachment to our past physical life focuses our attention on matter. The end result is that millions of people are energetically drawn to the lower dimensional levels that are close in frequency to the density of Earth. We experience what we focus our attention upon. This is why many influential teachers such as Buddha repeatedly emphasized the need for detachment from the physical. The key is to release the past and embrace your continuing adventures in the afterlife. How can we ever experience liberation and our ultimate spiritual potential when we remain focused on the density of earth?

What is the spiritual path?

We are multidimensional beings, and the spiritual path is the inner-dimensional journey of consciousness within us and leads to our reuniting with our spiritual source. Unknown to many, we exist as a microcosm of the entire multidimensional universe. When we shift our awareness inward through deep meditation, OBEs, and NDEs, we are experiencing and traveling the path within us. The expansive nonphysical nature of our multi-dimensional self is the universal spiritual path.

Why is knowledge of the afterlife so important in our transition at death?

Most of us were taught from birth that if we live a good life and have faith in a religious doctrine we automatically go to a heavenly paradise. Regrettably, this is a false assumption. At death a great majority of humanity enters a nonphysical energy dimension and reality existing just out of phase with the physical world. People are met by loved ones and are reunited in a very pleasant, physical-like environment. The many ills, pains, and harshness of the physical world are a thing of the past. There are no wars, starvation, or death in our new reality. The new environment appears perfect and pristine when compared to our past physical existence. At death most people settle for the first environment they experience. They remain unaware that countless other realities and dimensions are available that are far more magnificent and thought-responsive. The physical-like realities that most assume are the ultimate heaven are actually the epidermis of the continuum of dimensions that make up the multidimensional universe. By our own actions we have essentially settled for and accepted the energy reflections of Earth instead of the glorious realities of the higher-vibrational dimensions that are our true spiritual home. With spiritual development we gain the ability to enter and navigate the countless thought-responsive dimensions of the afterlife. Armed with self- knowledge, we become empowered. This is our destiny as an evolved soul.

Why is it so important to connect with our higher self?

The biblical concept of Heaven is actually the nonphysical interior of the multidimensional universe, consisting of countless energy dimensions and realities. Each individual will experience the nonphysical reality/heaven that resonates with them. Connecting with our higher self provides a considerable enhancement to our spiritual development. It allows us to open to and experience the divine source within us. Words are inadequate to describe the profound impact this merging would be to our spiritual evolution.

Can we access our past lives?

Yes. We carry all of our many life experiences with us; they remain deep within our subconscious mind. Through hypnosis and other altered states we can begin to access our other lives in different energy realities.

Do near-death experiences (NDEs) provide accurate information about the afterlife?

Having an NDE provides a glimpse into what may lie ahead for us after death. However, human perceptions are often distorted because they are framed by the belief system of the individual. The afterlife realities are extremely thought-responsive. For example, a Christian may perceive Jesus or angels, a Native American may see an animal spirit guide, and a person from India may see Yamraj—the Hindu king of the dead. It is important to note that NDEs have been proven to reduce or even eliminate fear in those that who had the experience. From this perspective it is very valuable. NDEs provide an extraordinarily special moment for someone, but do not assume you are receiving a complete picture of the afterlife based on this single brief experience.

What is nature of reality?

Consciousness creates reality. As a result, the universe is a multidimensional continuum of energies and the physical world is the outer epidermis layer (less than 1%). Each inner non-physical dimension we experience is progressively less dense and more thought-responsive. We exist as a consciousness microcosm of this vast energy continuum. The reality that we perceive and experience is determined by our state of consciousness and the density of the energy vehicle/body we are currently using for expression. All of the three dimensional environments that we experience are created and maintained by the collective consciousness of the local inhabitants.

Can I manifest anything I want in the afterlife?

This depends on your personal spiritual development and the nonphysical reality you are experiencing. You will most likely enter a consensus reality that will be as stable and real as the physical world. In <u>Adventures in the Afterlife</u>, Frank (the main character) could not change the first reality that he moved into. He could not alter it, even though he knew that there was something better. He was locked in a reality maintained by the collective thought (the consensus) of the inhabitants. As he expanded his awareness, he learned how to navigate the many diverse afterlife realities and effectively mold his reality.

What do you mean by the term spiritual mobility?

Most humans - both living and dead - are limited to a single dimensional reality. They are prisoners of their mind. Our spiritual mobility is our ability to consciously experience and traverse the inner expanse of our multidimensional self and obtain true freedom from the dense outer realities of form and matter.

Can I become a spiritual guide to others?

An important result of our enhanced self-knowledge and interdimensional mobility as soul is the privilege to assist others. The greater our spiritual awareness and mobility, the easier it will be to support our loved ones in the afterlife. Our ability to navigate effectively in the various nonphysical environments of the afterlife will allow us to provide valuable insight and assistance to those we encounter. If we choose, we can become a spiritual teacher sharing the knowledge we have acquired about the multidimensional nature of the spiritual universe. With our acquired interdimensional experience, we can become an effective guide to people both living and dead.

Can I assist my pet to make a spiritual transition?

Yes, we can assist our pets or other animals in their spiritual journey at death. We can provide the same support we would for any other loved one in our life.

I have not been able to have a conscious out-of-body experience (OBE). Does this mean I will not be able to reach my higher self at death?

Having an OBE is not a prerequisite for reaching your higher self during your transition. However, the same issues that are hindering your ability to have a conscious OBE could also deter you from reaching your spiritual goal at death.

I am an atheist. Can I still reunite with my higher self? Should I even try?

Yes, unchanging spiritual reality doesn't care what we believe or don't believe.

Why is developing our creative abilities so important to our afterlife?

All nonphysical realities are thought-responsive to some degree. The more that we develop our creative abilities and focus during our physical life, the greater will be our ability to influence and shape the thought-responsive environments we will experience in the afterlife.

How do I connect with my higher self?

There are many methods and approaches to the inner exploration of consciousness. Various forms of deep meditation practices are the most commonly used today. In addition, trance work, deep self-hypnosis, self-initiated and controlled OBEs, self-directed lucid dreaming, shamanic ceremony, various yoga methods, and even medicine plant journeys are all practiced. We are all different, so explore the various methods available and follow your intuition concerning what approach resonates with you. The key is to become an active spiritual explorer, instead of a passive believer of manmade doctrines.

What may occur during a spiritual experience?

Each individual perceives this profound experience differently. While having a spiritual experience the physical body often appears to be in a deeply relaxed state or trance. In general your awareness will shift inward and away from the physical senses. During the initial phases, vibrational or Kundalini phenomena (energy surges, inner sounds, and temporary paralysis) are often reported.

Common elements include trance-like states of consciousness, slowed breathing, and a distorted concept of time. Many report a feeling of weightlessness and a complete disassociation from the physical body. A perception of inner motion and a surge of energy through your body can be followed by vibrations or numbness. This shift will frequently manifest as an expanded state of consciousness that may include perception beyond the physical body.

The disassociation from the physical body and ego can lead to transcending the limits of time and space. Our perception expands beyond form-based images and is often highlighted by 360-degree vision. The connection to all existence is heightened and there is an overwhelming sense of pure love that can manifest as an ocean of light or a magnificent transcendent presence. Awareness of a completely nonphysical, non-form-based reality is often reported. An extensive examination of this experience is detailed in my first two books.

How should I respond to my shifts of consciousness?

First, remain calm; any sense of panic or thoughts of the body will bring you directly back to physical consciousness. Then, without fear, completely surrender to the inner vibrations, motion, lightness, or sounds and allow them to envelop your entire being. Accept these as natural and positive signs of a potential spiritual experience. All of these energy sensations are normal and indicate that a trance state is in process.

At this point you may have a sense of separation from your body; this could manifest as floating, sinking, or spinning. During deep trance states you can request to experience your spiritual self with firm affirmations such as, "Spiritual Essence Now," or "Higher Self Now!" Be completely open to the results and allow a perception of expansion, rapid inner movement, or any shift of consciousness that may follow. Enjoy your amazing journey. Refer to <u>Adventures beyond the Body</u> for more details and instruction.

What do you think about using a psychic medium to communicate with the dead?

There are some very intuitive psychics who can deliver messages from the afterlife. Be aware that any information you obtain will likely be highly influenced by the psychic's own mindset and viewpoints. The best way to receive feedback from your deceased loved one is through your own communication: meditation, trance states, and automatic writing, just to name a few. This can also be achieved through self-initiated lucid dreams and OBEs. For more information and personal accounts of those who have succeeded in contacting their loved ones, please refer to <u>The Secret of the Soul</u>.

Why does spiritual evolution seem to take so long?

The greatest block to our spiritual development is our continuing ignorance of our true self. Let's face a stark reality—the vast majority of people don't know the basics of their existence: what am I, what's my purpose, where we are going at death, where did I come from before my birth, what is the nature of reality, and what is the afterlife? This complete absence of self-knowledge opens the door to an overwhelming dependency on narrow theories and beliefs. The lack of spiritual self-knowledge leads to the indoctrination and manipulation of the masses. When ignorant of our true spiritual existence - wars, murder, and inhumanity are the result. Filling the void, institutional belief systems prosper as they continue to distort the reality of our spiritual existence and our multidimensional path as soul.

However, we can change this today; a single profound spiritual experience can radically transform your entire perception of reality. Suddenly you know you are an immortal being and that you are connected to all that is. You absolutely know that you continue beyond the physical and you realize that you are fully accountable for your actions. When you personally experience your spiritual nature you truly know—not just believe—that all harmful acts directed against another are only harming you. Your awakening is everything.

Do souls go to everlasting biblical heaven at death?

The popular belief that we automatically enter some mythic everlasting heaven at death is inaccurate. The biblical heaven is actually the vast multidimensional universe. We are immortal, nonphysical beings; at death we shed our outer dense body and enter the energy dimension that resonates with our current state of consciousness and spiritual development. Most humans reunite with their loved ones and experience a pleasant physical-like reality located within the astral dimension. Based upon decades of exploration countless afterlife environments and realities (heavens) exist within a series of nonphysical energy dimensions. Our evolution as soul is centered on change and growth in multiple dimensional realities.

Why are our spiritual affirmations so important during the process of death?

A mindset focused on our highest spiritual intention can assist us to achieve our stated goal. Repeated affirmations are one of the most effective and universal methods to saturate our mind and achieve our focused intention. Our focused spiritual intention can enhance our individual frequency rate and our state of consciousness assisting us to potentially access higher-vibrational realities after death. "Higher Self Now!"

How and why is communication with the departed experienced?

A departed soul can communicate with the living through dreams and OBEs. It is also possible to receive a message through a third party such as a psychic medium or clairaudient intuitive. Automatic writing, visions, and meditation all provide an avenue for the departed to send messages to you. People connect with their deceased loved ones for two primary reasons. First, they want some form of verification that their friend or family member is doing well and that they will someday be able to reunite. Another reason is an unresolved issue such as an apology or a word of gratitude that was never spoken during the physical relationship.

What is your interpretation of the Buddhist approach to awakening in life and death, specifically the Eight Fold Path?

The core concepts of Buddhism are The Four Noble Truths and The Eightfold Path. They are essentially the same through every sect and tradition of Buddhism and were originally taught by Gautama Buddha about 2500 years ago. This information may be helpful as we develop our personal spiritual practice and our spiritual directive. The following is my personal interpretation. Please contact your local Buddhist organization for comprehensive information concerning Buddhist philosophies and/or ceremonies.

THE FOUR NOBLE TRUTHS

- All life knows suffering. Life can be extremely challenging and even painful at times.
- The cause of suffering is ignorance and clinging. Recognize that the constant need to acquire possessions will not create peace of mind or lasting personal fulfillment.
- There is a way to end human suffering. Realize that all physical things and conditions are a temporary reality. Learn not to cling to the physical show and its constant drama.
- The Eightfold Path is a way to end suffering and achieve peace of mind.

THE EIGHTFOLD PATH

Right Understanding: Learn about the nature of reality, the truth about your existence and your path through life.

Right Aspiration: Make a personal commitment to live and think in such a way that suffering can end.

Right Effort: Just Do It. No excuses.

Right Speech: Speak the truth in a helpful and compassionate way.

Right Conduct: Live your life consistent with your highest ideals; doing no harm to others.

Right Livelihood: Earn an honest living in a way that doesn't harm others.

Right Mindfulness: Recognize the value of calming the rambling mind and focusing on the present moment.

Right Concentration: Explore and expand your consciousness through meditation.

Remembering that our state of consciousness is the only possession we will take with us at death is an important realization. As explorers, it's essential that we protect and develop our only valuable asset.

Questions and Comments

Part Two

What is Hospice?

HOSPICE IS A philosophy and care plan that is directed toward providing dignity and comfort to the dying and their families. It is based on a team effort and can be provided in the home or a facility. A patient under hospice care will have a specific medical treatment path that supports that philosophy.

When should we consider hospice care for our loved one?

The primary reason for hospice care is professional assistance and care. There are specific requirements from your health insurance and/or Medicare policy regarding eligibility that you may have to follow. This can be discussed with your doctor or social worker. Consider what hospice care is and then make a decision based on your individual need. The team assigned to you can support you with education and training to take the guesswork out of your home care. Counselors become available to you to assist with social issues and grief. Volunteers offer to provide respite for caregivers. Hospice is as much for the family as it is for the patient. Discuss it with your current medical provider and together you can develop the timing plan that works for you.

What is another good reason to use the services of a hospice?

When a patient dies at home under hospice care, the nurse can pronounce death in a peaceful atmosphere that supports a focused spiritual transition. There is no need to call 911 and witness the potential resuscitation efforts that will follow. Depending on the circumstances, there could be a mandatory transport to the local hospital, police involvement, and delays in releasing the body to you. First responders will be doing their job exactly as they are required to do for all reports of a death. If you have a terminally ill diagnosis and take your last breath in a natural succession of the disease, the hospice team can eliminate the need for this dramatic sequence of events.

Why should I consider a hospice facility instead of keeping my loved one at home?

Most people would rather spend their last days at home, but sometimes it is more practical to be in a place that has professional care and equipment. There might be a need for specialized attention that is not realistic to manage at home. Pain management is another reason that someone might be more comfortable in a medical setting. Medications can be administered to best meet the comfort needs of the patient. Often the primary caregiver cannot physically manage the needs of their loved one. This is especially true with an elderly spouse or partner.

In addition, some people are afraid of making a mistake that could harm their loved one. After all, most of us do not have a professional health background and it can be quite scary to be the one to administer medication or work with medical equipment if you have never done it before.

One of the most touching reasons that I have seen is the person that wants to turn over all medical care to professionals so that they can focus 100% of their efforts on the spiritual and emotional needs of their friend or family member.

What is the difference between palliative care and curative care?

Palliative care is providing comfort to the seriously ill. This may or may not be a terminal diagnosis, but there is no attempt to cure a disease with this type of care. The goal is provide quality-of-life improvements for the patient. This includes pain relief, emotional support, help with symptoms, and alternative therapies. Conversely, curative care is designed to address the underlying disease with the goal of eliminating it.

I've heard that some people are critical of hospice. Why do you think that is?

Sometimes expectations do not meet reality. Many times people are overwhelmed with all the paperwork, legal requirements, and medical terminology on top of their raw emotional distress.

It's no wonder that they become confused with the role of the hospice and the people who support their care. As an example, if you ask a technician about medication, you may not get an immediate answer and this can be frustrating to someone unfamiliar with team roles and responsibilities. This is why I always encourage you to educate yourself before it becomes a medical necessity.

Second, there may be an underlying emotional issue that manifests as anger towards the institution. Perhaps there is some guilt involved if a family member is unable to care for the loved one on their own. A secondary participant may be angry about the cost of care and how it affects their inheritance. The feeling of helplessness as you watch someone die while you are unable to stop it can cause misplaced frustration.

A third reason might be that people fail to take personal responsibility. There is an expectation in the hospice world that friends and families continue to support the dying from a psychological-comfort perspective. It is not realistic to expect that all spiritual and emotional needs can be successfully delegated to others. The best care you can provide is still personal, supplemented by the hospice team.

In the end, hospice is a personal choice. One of my functions as a volunteer in one facility is to accumulate the feedback from families and friends who have used our service. The overwhelming majority are very thankful that there was a team in place to help them through the most difficult moments. They truly appreciate the respect and dignity that is afforded the patient in the last days of life.

My sister-in-law was just released from a hospice facility. Were the doctors wrong about her illness?

Hospice is generally recommended for those who have a prognosis of less than six months to live. Sometimes it is difficult to predict without question exactly how long someone will live with the disease or medical condition. After six months in hospice, a patient is re-evaluated to determine the proper course of continuing care. Some will remain under hospice and some will transfer to a different level of care. I have seen people 'graduate' from hospice and either go home or move to an assisted-living facility. This does not mean that the medical team has made a mistake, only that the disease is progressing at a different rate than originally expected.

Why can't I continue to feed my brother in hospice?

As people are dying, their body functions begin to slow down in order to preserve energy. The digestive system is one of the early processes that will stop. If you continue to feed someone in this state, they will feel worse because undigested food sits in their body with nowhere to go. This can cause discomfort, vomiting, and even choking. Follow the direction of the medical team when it comes to food. They are not trying to starve your brother; they are dedicated to keeping him comfortable.

Why do some dying people, like my father, linger for extensive periods of time? Can I assist?

Each person will die on their own schedule. Some of the reasons that someone might 'hang on' are:

- Perhaps there is an event that he doesn't want to miss. Is there a graduation, birth, or anniversary in the near future? Your father may want to be there and have that experience before he passes.
- From a practical standpoint, it could be the natural progression of disease. The physical changes are happening at a slower pace than you anticipated.
- Is there a goal that he has yet to achieve? Maybe he simply needs to finish writing his life story.
- It is difficult to grant forgiveness, but there could be someone he needs to see in order to have reconciliation.

You can support your father's mission by asking some open questions. "Is there anything I can help you to achieve in these last days/weeks?" "Can I call anyone to come for a visit?" "Are you worried about anyone/anything?" "What concerns you the most right now?" The important part of any conversation is to emphasize that you are there for whatever he needs to make his journey peaceful.

How does Reiki help a person who is dying?

There is an energy field that is an integral part of our physical body. When a trained practitioner uses their hands on or above the physical body, it can rebalance the energy field, bringing comfort to the patient. This practice can provide pain relief and ease extreme emotions.

Many hospice locations will offer Reiki to the family and the facility staff as well. It has been shown to provide benefits in reducing anxiety and the physical symptoms that often accompany a high-stress situation.

Is there anything special I should do to prepare before I visit a dying friend?

There are a few things you can do to support the right mindset when visiting someone who has a limited time. This starts before you enter the room.

- Talk to a close family member so you know if there are any out-of-bounds topics. Maybe the family doesn't want the patient to know that another loved one is terminally ill. Perhaps finances are strained due to medical costs, but that isn't a burden that needs to be placed on the dying.

- It is also good to know what to expect in terms of physical changes. If you haven't seen this person in a year, you might be surprised at the weight loss or muscle weakness of your previously healthy friend. The look of shock on your face might be a disturbing sight.

- Keep your own mind clear. Try to shake off any troubles or concerns of your own before entering the room. Sometimes, I picture myself in a shower stall with warm water washing away the issues of my day so that I have an uncluttered mind before a visit. Remember to focus on support for your friend by asking about their level of comfort and emotional well-being.

- In nervous chatter I have heard people complaining about something rather minor in relation to the person lying in the bed. It might help to have some conversation thought-starters before you enter the room.

The bottom line is to arrive with a spirit of love and support. That will show through to your friend even if you think you've said the wrong thing (and we all think we have at some point.) The fact that you have taken time to be there is the most important component.

What should I say if someone asks me if they are dying?

This depends on your relationship with the patient. As a volunteer, I would probably say something like, "What does your medical team say about that?" and follow the conversation from there. As a co-worker or more distant friend or relative, I would be even less specific because I would not want to contradict or be inconsistent with the family directive. "I don't know the specifics of your situation. I'm sure you can discuss that with your family/doctor/faith community. I'm here to see how you are feeling and if there is anything I can do for you."

If the person is a close loved one and you are the caregiver or most responsible person in the picture, you can be more direct. Here are some potential scenarios depending on your rapport with the patient.

- "You have been fighting this terrible disease for some time now. I'm sorry to say that the doctors have exhausted all treatments that would improve your condition. So the answer is yes. Our goal now is to make you as comfortable as possible."
- "Do you feel like you are dying? Are you in pain or anxious in any way?"
- "What can I do to ease your fears about death?"
- "Yes, your physical time here is limited. Considering that, is there anything I should know that will help you make this transition?"
- "Would you like to tell me about what you are feeling right now?"

Bear in mind that if someone asks this question, they probably already know that they are dying and are just looking for validation. Before you provide it, make sure that it is appropriate, based on your relationship, to deliver such a confirmation.

Don't all people know that they are dying?

Most people have a moment of clarity where they realize what is happening to their physical body. However, there are a few exceptions. Some parents do not want to talk about death to a child who has a life-limiting illness (even though the child may know what is happening). There are cases where Mom doesn't want the word 'cancer' or 'hospice' or 'dying' mentioned in the home. This is a denial tactic that really serves no purpose, but it is the choice of the family. Another example is the wife that doesn't want her husband to give up hope, so she will not acknowledge the truth of the situation. The patient may know they are dying, but they don't want to disappoint family members who appear to have not given up. Maintaining this lie is a waste of energy, but more importantly it is a lost opportunity to assist someone in their spiritual transition.

I cannot travel to visit my aunt who is dying from breast cancer. She is unconscious most of the time and I will feel guilty if I don't do something. Do you have any suggestions?

You don't have to be physically present to provide comfort to a dying loved one. Contact someone who is able to visit. Set up a time and ask them to call you. Hold the phone to your aunt's ear and speak in a normal tone. Tell her who you are, and that you love her and wish her well on her journey. Depending on how close you were, you could thank her for something specific, relate to a favorite memory, or provide some affirmations. All evidence shows that, in this state, people can still hear. Although they may not respond to your comments, you can be assured that they are taking in your kind words.

Should I bring my children in to visit their dying grandfather?

Of course this depends on the age and maturity of the child, but here are some things to consider when making this decision. Death is a natural part of life. Sheltering or deceiving children from this event could have a negative impact on the way they look at death in the future. Eventually they will know the truth. That being said, it isn't necessary to go through all the details about the disease. A simple explanation that the grandparent is dying and will soon move on from the physical world should be enough. If the child asks questions, you should answer as honestly as possible. I would recommend talking to the child prior to entering the room so they are not frightened by a change in appearance or energy level.

Children are seeing death on a daily basis through TV shows, video games, and news reports. This view should be balanced with the reality of dying so that they can develop a sense of respect for the process.

My husband is afraid that he will feel pain. What can I say to reassure him?

Assuming a gradual death under the care of hospice, pain medication will continue until your last breath. There is no reason to think that anyone is in pain at that time. Looking at facial expressions will give you a clue as to someone's level of comfort. A grimace, moan, or abnormal eye movements may be part of life processing, but can be interpreted as physical pain. To be certain, consult your medical team.

When removing life support, you can request pain medication for your loved one. This will give you peace of mind that discomfort is not a factor during the transition. In your discussions with your family, you should make your thoughts on pain medication during a terminal illness clear and legally documented. Remember, pain can bind a person to their body, making it more difficult to focus on a meaningful spiritual transition.

Should I continue affirmations and visualizations when my loved one is sleeping, unresponsive, or even comatose?

Yes, because hearing is the last sense to be dimmed. Hospice workers always assume that the patient can continue to hear after sight and speech have diminished. Even after death, the soul may still be present making final adjustments. This is why some cultures continue their spiritual verbal guidance by chanting even after the last breath to help direct the soul who is making a transition.

What about patients with dementia? Can they still benefit from hearing affirmations?

First, let's clarify the meaning of dementia. This is not a disease in itself, but a grouping of symptoms that indicate a decline in mental ability. There are a variety of causes for this impairment including, but not limited to, the most common type—Alzheimer's disease. The symptoms cover a wide spectrum of severity, so it would be difficult to gauge where someone is in the progression of this condition. And because this is a physical disorder it can be a separate condition from that of the soul. The subconscious mind may very well be functioning adequately, so there may be a response to the affirmations even if reasoning or judgment has diminished. Any recorded information played for someone who has lost some communications skills can only help in their spiritual transition in the last days of life. I would continue to use these tools for as long as your intuition tells you.

What should I do if my friend starts to hallucinate and see things that I don't see?

Visions of the previously departed are very common as one approaches death. To your friend, this is not a hallucination but a very real occurrence. You should support it as such. It's OK to ask questions, but know when to drop the subject if he does not want to continue talking about it. Some people mean well, but have placed their own limitations on someone else's experience by trying to explain away visions as an effect of drugs or the spread of disease.

Your friend may also begin to see glimpses of his next destination by way of tunnels, lights, fields, or forests. There may be references to train stations, airports, or highways. All of this is very natural and should be expected rather than dismissed as a hallucination. Make supportive comments such as, "Tell me more about what you see." Or "What do you think that means?" This can help your friend explore his next conscious experience.

The nurse told me that my friend is actively dying. What does that mean?

Everyone dies a little differently, but there are common conditions that indicate death is imminent. These involve, but are not limited to, changes in blood pressure, body temperature, breathing, and waste output. Skin color in the extremities can change due to a variation in oxygen and blood flow. You won't even see many of these changes, but the nurse will monitor them for you. What you will see is a condition where your friend appears to be sleeping all of the time. She will probably not make any sounds or acknowledge your presence. Her eyes may be constantly open or closed with little or no blinking. As she breathes, air flow will become progressively more spaced out until the last one is taken. After a few moments, a nurse will verify her death by checking heartbeat, pulse points, and breathing.

What are reasons to consider a doula?

Having a doula available can eliminate some fears that may not become apparent during the initial stages of a terminal illness. Most families can rally together in times of crisis and be very successful until the days/hours prior to death. Maybe there is a pretty good routine in place, but then the condition changes. A doula can be an information messenger between your family and the medical team when you are too overwrought to communicate clearly. Some families do not want to observe any perceived (or real) suffering at the end, but don't want their loved one to be alone either. This is a situation where a doula can be the final companion.

Others just do not want to be alone in the home when the end comes. It is comforting to know that someone will be there to help you through the extreme emotional wave that you may experience. A doula with spiritual knowledge can assist you with affirmations, music, and prayer to support the soul as it moves to the higher self. Also, the logistics at the time of death can be handled by a doula so that you can focus on the calm transition of your loved one.

You talk about comforting someone who has recently had a loss. Are there some comments that I should not make?

Talking to someone who is grieving can put even a confident person at a loss for words. If this is the case, most people will fall back to clichés or comments that they think will help their friend 'get over' their grief. So here are some examples that are not helpful.

- *"It was his time."* You are not in a position to make a judgment or prediction about when anyone's time is up.
- *"He's in a better place."* You do not know where he is or whether it is a better place. This is not only making an assumption about someone's belief system, but I'm sure the saddened family member would think that right there with them is a better place.
- *"Don't be sad."* It is not appropriate to tell someone how they should be feeling. Not only have they lost someone very close to them, but now their friends are invalidating how they feel about it.

- *"You are still young. You can have another baby."* No one can exchange a lost child with another one. This comment demeans the first child as if they can be easily replaced.
- *"It's been six months. You should be over it. Get out there and meet someone new."* There is no timetable for grief. Everyone has a different process. Be a supportive friend without making them feel bad about their behavior. Do not pressure someone into an activity that they are not ready for.
- *"Oh, well. We all have to die sometime."* This is true. But you didn't die.
- *"My brother lost his wife last year and he still isn't over it. You'll probably be crying for months. I'm just letting you know what's going to happen."* No two people grieve exactly alike. Give someone space to explore their feelings. And don't be critical if they haven't been sad as long as you think they should be.
- *"When will you start dating again? Are you going to stay in your house? What will you do with the second car?"* A grieving person has probably not yet considered these plans and even if they have, most likely it's not your business. Keep your conversation supportive rather than inquisitive.

The best thing to say is something simple and from your heart. For example: "I'm sorry. I know you loved him very much. We'll all miss him. Is there anything I can do for you or the children?" I lost one of my home visit patients rather unexpectedly. I had grown quite fond of him, so the news of Mark's death was a surprisingly hurtful for me. At his funeral, I was a little choked up. I embraced his sister and just said "There are no words." When in doubt, a gentle hug is usually welcomed.

When I hear about a plane crash or natural disaster I feel the need to help. How can I provide transition assistance to those I have never even met?

We can assist others from a distance. Because we may not know them personally, I would suggest some basic affirmations used during a meditative or prayerful state of consciousness. As you enter this mindset, visualize the incident and try to create a mental picture of those people who may have lost their physical body during the event. Repeat these affirmations, either silently or out loud:

You are safe, returning to the source
You are flowing in the path of light
You embrace the flow of your spiritual essence
You are on your way home
You have unlimited energy to follow your spiritual path
You are easily moving along the journey to spiritual enlightenment
You joyfully go to the clear light of your source
You are surrounded by love moving along your spiritual path
You separate from the physical to consciously become your higher self

Do not be surprised if you can feel the energy of someone in transition during these affirmations. You may be reaching a lost soul who is in need of some direction.

Terms

Actively Dying – This is the term used to describe a person who is in the final stages of physical life. There may be just days or hours left before the last breath. Certain physical attributes are present that lead the medical team to this conclusion.

Advanced Medical Directive – Specifies who can make medical decisions for you if you become physically or mentally incapacitated. This term is interchangeable with Medical Power of Attorney, Health Care Surrogate, or Health Care Power of Attorney depending on your state. (Please seek legal advice for more information. Specifics can differ by state.)

Bardo – The Buddhist phrase for the many thought created realities of the physical and nonphysical dimensions. Commonly thought to be the thought responsive realities we experience immediately after death. I often use the term 'consensus reality' to convey the same basic concept.

Chakras – This is a Sanskrit word meaning wheel or circle. These energy centers in the subtle body are generally thought to hold spiritual and health significance. The seven main locations from the top of the head down are: crown, third eye, throat, heart, solar plexus, sacral, and root.

Clairaudient (Clear Hearing) – The ability to hear guidance for yourself or others through channeling, listening to your inner voice, or receiving message from your spirit guides.

Claircognizant (Clear Knowing) – This is the source of inspired ideas, creative insights, or information that seemingly appear from nowhere.

Clairsentient (Clear Feeling) – Using your intuition, energy fields, gut feelings, and emotions to provide assistance for any situations in your life. This could also include physical sensations, unusual smells, or tastes that trigger a connection to something unique for you.

Clairvoyant (Clear Seeing) – The ability to receive messages through visual images perceived through either physical or nonphysical perception.

Clear Light of the Void – A Buddhist phrase that refers to a higher vibrational dimension of reality existing beyond all form-based constructs. In Buddhist philosophy going to the Clear Light immediately at death can lead to liberation from the bardos (the consensus realities) and provide potential freedom from the educational process of reincarnation.

Consciousness – A common term for soul. Our core awareness and being that exists beyond all form, thought and energy constructs.

Consensus Reality – Any reality or environment created and maintained by the collective thoughts of the inhabitants. These environments are structurally stable and resistant to individual thought. After death most humans enter consensus nonphysical realities that resonate with their personal development and beliefs.

Construct – Any form-based reality, body or environment created by thought. The physical and astral worlds are constructs shaped and molded by group consciousness. The energy body we experience in every dimension is a construct of our consciousness. All constructs are temporary creations of individual or collective consciousness.

Cremation – A process using high temperatures, vaporization, and oxidation to change the physical body to ashes.

Crisis Apparition – Many people report seeing or hearing a loved one shortly after a death has occurred, even when there is physical distance between the deceased and the observer. The soul can temporarily visit the physical world for a brief goodbye that can provide closure to the relationship. This form can be a hazy outline, exceptionally bright, or clear and defined in a younger, healthier 'body.' If an individual dies with unfinished business, this is one way for it to provide a final message to the living.

Deathbed Visions – During the last days of life, a dying person will often begin to see beings and personalities from the other side. These can be familiar faces, friends or family members who have previously died, or a guide who has come to assist the soul's passing. These visions are very common and rarely create any fear in the person who is having them.

Doula – An end-of-life doula is a companion to the actively dying. Other terms are transition coach and end-of-life coach. This person (or team) is generally not in the medical profession, but a trusted member of your spiritual organization, a volunteer from hospice or other medical facility, or even a family friend. The primary purpose is to provide comfort and companionship to the dying, but they can also be a liaison between the family and medical team if required.

Empath – Someone who can strongly sense or is affected by the energies of other people is said to have empathetic qualities. They can sense the motives, emotions, and intentions of others, sometimes so deeply that it has an impact on their own moods.

Escape Velocity – This a phrase coined by Robert Monroe; the concept of achieving liberation of consciousness from the repetition of the Earth life reality training and educational system.

Executor – This is a person who has been legally assigned to see that instructions from your will are carried out in an honest and timely manner. They will pay debts and taxes owed by the estate and dispose of remaining property and assets as documented. It is the responsibility of the executor to perform such tasks as locating assets, contacting beneficiaries, obtaining death certificates, closing credit cards, and notifying organizations such as the Social Security Administration, insurance companies, and others that have financial connections to the deceased. (Please seek legal advice for more information. Specifics can differ by state.)

Higher Self – Our eternal spiritual essence or true self existing beyond all form-based concepts and thought. It is the part of you that has knowledge of your past lives, your current mission, and your path beyond matter. It is the seat of your pure spiritual self. Our higher self uses many different vibrational energy bodies in multiple dimensions for expression, exploration and spiritual evolution.

Hospice – The hospice philosophy and practice provides end-of-life care to both the patient and their family. Typically hospice is suggested by a panel of doctors when someone is determined to have less than six months to live. This support can be provided in a person's home, in a hospice facility, or in a medical care facility. There will be a team of health care professionals, volunteers, counselors, and others dedicated to providing comfort to the dying and support for their families. Medical staff will provide care that allows the patient to remain alert and comfortable until the end of life.

Living Will – This is a document used to capture your wishes with regard to medical procedures that you want or do not want if your health is at a point where you cannot verbalize your choices. It allows you to name an advocate for your health care needs. (Please seek legal advice for more information. Specifics can differ by state.)

Palliative Care – This is specialized medical care for those with a serious (but not necessarily terminal) illness. The focus is on providing relief for symptoms including pain and stress to improve the quality of life for both the patient and their family.

Power of Attorney (POA) – This process allows you to name someone that you wish to represent you in financial and medical matters. A financial POA can pay bills, access your banking information, and handle tax accounts. A medical POA will be able to make medical decisions on your behalf in case of physical or mental incapacitation. If the POA is identified as *Durable*, then they have immediate financial authority and that remains in effect even after a medical authority/court identifies you as incapacitated. A *Limited* Power of Attorney document generally is written to address a specific concern such as a real estate transaction. (Please seek legal advice for more information. Specifics can differ by state.)

Reiki –A method for connecting universal energy to the healing power of one's own physical body through the use of hands placed on or above the body.

Shared Death Experience – A term coined by Raymond Moody to describe a shared consciousness with someone during the process and transition of death. It is said to be used to show a close friend or family member the transition environment, and is a gift of reassurance that death is not the end.

Smudging – This is a Native American spiritual cleansing technique that involves burning specific herbs for spiritual and emotional purification related to a person, place, or object.

Spiritual Directive – This was created by William Buhlman to document and communicate the spiritual desires of an individual during their transition. Unlike a will created to divide assets at death, this is meant strictly to address specific spiritual intentions and goals. It is a detailed action plan for the spiritual transition of consciousness during the process of death.

Spiritual Release Ceremony – When someone has just died they may benefit from a ceremony where friends, family members, or community spiritual leaders verbalize their desire to see the soul move on to the next plane. Some examples of these are cited in Chapter 7, "Creating a Sacred Space and Time." This can also be used if time has lapsed but the spirit seems to be having trouble moving beyond the physical world.

Thanatology – Thanatology is the study of death and dying that includes the mechanics and forensics of death (i.e., bodily changes) as well as attitudes and behaviors related to death, grief, and mourning.

Transition – A popular term for death of the physical body.

Water Ceremony – Many cultures use water in the cleansing and purification of the mind, spirit, and/or body. This usually includes a prayer and ritual activity. Some cultures will also include flowers, plants, or herbs. The following terms outline some different process definitions in a water ceremony.

- Ablution – washing of one's body as a spiritual act
- Aspersion – the scattering and sprinkling of water
- Immersion – merging or plunging into the liquid
- Libation – pouring as an offering and then consuming
- Purification – cleansing for the sake of purity

A Buddhist Perspective on Death

Centuries ago, the concept of a thought-responsive afterlife was presented in the revered book, <u>The Tibetan Book of the Dead</u>. Unfortunately, few in the western world have taken the time to study the importance or meaning of the texts. For many of us, the instruction is obscured by the unfamiliar Buddhist phrasing and terms. From my perspective I have listed some basic guidance to help clarify the core teaching.

During the process of dying:

- Renounce all attachments. Recognize that the physical body is an illusion. Release all attachments to the physical world and your body.
- Place your attention at the top of your head (crown chakra).
- Remain focused on your Buddha nature (your spiritual essence) during the entire process of dying.
- Focus your mind on the clear light of the void (beyond all form-based realities) and your highest intention.
- Do not stop at the afterlife intermediate states or bardos. (What I would describe as the thought created realities that dominate the astral dimension.)
- Do not be hindered or side tracked by images or manifestations of fear or pleasure (wrathful, peaceful or sensual deities). Continue to focus on your highest spiritual intention (your Buddha nature).
- Have an experienced Buddhist lama or monk at your death bed to provide assistance at death and beyond. Ideally, this is a skilled monk who can perform the Phowa ceremony.

- When possible, perform a daily release ceremony for up to 49 days to assist your loved one in their progression through the various thought responsive realities or bardos of the afterlife.
- Practice cremation of the body to break all remaining attachments to the physical world.

Here are a few of the fundamental statements that are incorporated during a Buddhist ceremony as physical death becomes imminent.

- I remember my core teachings.
- I no longer need worldly involvement or engagements. I release all attachments to my physical body and the physical world.
- I will abandon all attachments and focus my mind on *the Buddha of Infinite Light* (my essence).
- I am going to transfer my consciousness and no obstacle will block my way to the *Pure Land of Infinite light*. (clear light)
- Therefore I am going to pray (meditate). I am focusing my mind strongly on my highest intention (My Buddha nature).
- I experience/unite with my Buddha nature (my Higher Self).

Affirmations can be recorded and played by the bedside of a dying loved one. Today many people are creating customized audio programs for themselves to support their personal spiritual traditions and goals.

Please contact your local Buddhist organization for detailed instruction on the teachings of Buddhism and their perspective on assisting someone during transition.

Informational Resources

BOOKS
<u>On Life after Death</u>
By: Elizabeth Kubler-Ross, MD
"A small book of four classic essays based on the doctor's studies of more than twenty-thousand people who have had near-death experiences. Included are her sensitive, original, and even controversial findings on death, dying, and the afterlife."

<u>Adventures in the Afterlife</u>
By: William Buhlman
"A unique and mind expanding exploration of the afterlife based upon the personal experiences of the author. After a terminal illness takes the life of the main character, Frank Brooks, the reader is treated to an uplifting spiritual journey into multiple realities and spiritual training environments existing within the afterlife."

<u>The Art of Comforting</u>
By: Val Walker
"This warm and engaging book is full of practical suggestions for all those who suddenly find themselves in the role of 'comforter' as well as for the professional nurturers among us."

Far Journeys
By: Robert Monroe
"This is a classic work that dives deep into the exploration of nonphysical realities and consciousness."

Final Gifts
By: Maggie Callahan and Patricia Kelley
"For more than a decade these hospice nurses have tended the terminally ill. In this moving and compassionate book, they share their intimate experiences with patients at the end of life."

Handbook to the Afterlife
By: Pamela Rae Heath and Jon Klimo
"...an overview that summarizes human thought and feeling, fear and faith. The book speaks clearly to all who question: "What happens to me after I die?"

The Holographic Universe
By: Michael Talbot
"This is a well written presentation concerning the multidimensional nature of reality from a scientific view point."

The Tibetan Book of the Dead
First Complete Translation
Penguin Books
"The classic composed by Padmasambhava with an introduction by The Dalai Lama."

Prelude to Eternity
By: Anne Pennington Grenfell

"This is an intimate, moving and compelling portrait of a couple's travels through life's greatest challenge: preparing for its ending. The story offers convincing evidence that physical death is just a preface to the next level of existence."

The Tibetan Book of Living and Dying
By: Sogyal Rinpoche
"This text is a clear-eyed and contemporary exploration of the profound insights found in Buddhism." *This is one of my personal favorites.*

Reiki Energy Medicine: Bringing Healing Touch into Home, Hospital and Hospice
By: Libby Barnett and Maggie Babb, with Susan Davidson
"...presents a simple, effective, and ancient method through which the natural healing potential of the body can be stimulated, enhancing the efficacy of conventional treatment."

After Death Communication, Final Farewells
By: Louis E. LA Grand, Ph.D.
"Extraordinary experiences of those mourning the death of loved ones."

Heading Toward Omega
By: Dr. Kenneth Ring
"It breaks new ground in the field of near-death studies by focusing on the meaning of the near-death experience for the survivor and for human evolution."

Beyond Past Lives
By: Mira Kelley

"This is about what parallel realities can teach us about relationships, healing, and transformation."

The Secret of the Soul
By William Buhlman
"This is an extensive examination into OBEs, the nature of reality and our afterlife journey. The two hundred OBE examples and experiences are based upon feedback obtained from 16,000 survey responses over twelve years."

WEBSITES
All websites listed here were active and functional at the time this book was printed. As with anything from the web, please use your judgment and due diligence when reviewing the information. By listing these sites, we are not endorsing any organization, product, or program, merely providing some alternative resources.

HOSPICE AND SUPPORT
www.gonefrommysight.com
Hosted by Barbara Karnes, this blog has pertinent information based on many years of hospice nursing experience.
www.accompanyingthedying.com
This is a site offering doula training as a profession.
www.mourningdoula.com
Here you will find a variety of interview questions should you decide to hire a professional doula.
www.nhpco.org
This is the site for the National Hospice and Palliative Care Organization. There is good information here if you are considering a hospice plan for yourself or loved one.

STATE-BY-STATE INFORMATION

www.deathwithdignity.org

Here is where you can find the latest "right to die" legislation by state.

www.caringinfo.org

Linked to this site are downloads of advanced directives by state.

www.deathcafe.com

This site will provide information about death cafes and direct you to a group in your area.

HEALTH AND WELLNESS

www.monroeinstitute.org

The Monroe Institute is a highly regarded organization dedicated to the exploration of consciousness through education and workshops.

www.reikirays.com

Several experienced Reiki professionals contribute to this blog.

www.reiki.org

This is a location for information, instruction and resources for Reiki.

www.ancienthuna.com

This site explains in detail the Huna process of Ho'oponopono.

www.afsp.org

This is the site for The American Foundation for Suicide Prevention.

www.sevenponds.com

This is an outlet that promotes an open dialogue about death. Some of the sections on this site include an after-death planning guide that addresses practical aspects such as estate planning and consumer rights regarding commercial funeral services.

MEMORIALS AND FUNERALS

www.homefuneralalliance.org
A site dedicated to the art of the home funeral.
www.greenburialcouncil.org
This council provides a certification for green funerals and burials as well as providing education and advocacy for the consumer.
www.eternalreefs.com
This company offers an eco-friendly alternative to burial by creating an artificial reef ball and placing it in an EPA-approved location to support local sea life.
www.cremationsolutions.com
The EPA recommends this site as a resource for rules and regulations regarding the spreading of ashes. Although it is a commercial site, if you check in the footnote/informational section, you will see laws and regulations for scattering ashes.

GRIEF

www.nationalallianceforgrievingchildren.org
This site will help you to find support in your area along with information about the grieving process for children. This organization also sponsors an annual symposium with workshops and lectures addressing the topic.
www.pet-loss.net
This site will help you to navigate through the emotions related to pet loss, conquering associated guilt, and helping children cope. There is a guide that will help you find a pet cemetery by state location.
www.recover-from-grief.com

This is a place where you can find grief education resources, tips for survival, advice for grieving kids, pet loss, and forums for readers to share their grief experiences.

www.mindfulnessandgrief.com

With a Master's degree in Thanatology, this blogger has created a site dedicated to lessening grief through meditation, yoga and journaling. There are some guided meditations here that could be helpful.

The Monroe Institute

The Monroe Institute (TMI) is a preeminent leader in human consciousness exploration. TMI is devoted to the premise that focused consciousness contains the answers to humankind's questions. Through the use of technology, education, research and development, TMI has been advancing the experience of individuals in the exploration of targeted and expanded states of awareness for over 40 years.

TMI program participants learn experientially through a specially designed audio-guidance system at a 450-acre residential retreat nestled in Virginia's scenic Blue Ridge Mountains, just outside Charlottesville's city limits. Founded in the early 1970s as an educational and research organization by inventor and sound pioneer Robert Monroe, TMI offers numerous week-long and week-end residential programs every year on the main campus in Faber, Virginia, and over 200 programs throughout the U.S., Europe, Latin America and Asia. The centerpiece of TMI learning is the guided use of Hemi-Sync® audio technologies created by Robert Monroe more than 40 years ago and used by millions. For more information and class schedules, please visit their website: www.monroeinstitute.org.

William Buhlman Workshops at the Monroe Institute

OUT-OF-BODY EXPLORATION INTENSIVE WORKSHOP
This exciting workshop focuses on effective OBE preparation, induction, separation methods and control techniques. Each workshop is based upon William's four decades of personal experience and is highly experiential, practical and inspirational. Over the course of this unique program you will experience extensive step-by-step exercises, tips, techniques, and answers to your every question about out-of-body exploration. This is a unique opportunity to interact with like-minded people in a fun and positive atmosphere. Out-of-body exploration techniques will be practiced in the famous CHEC units.

DURING THIS EMPOWERING WORKSHOP YOU WILL EXPERIENCE:

- Extensive out-of-body and inner exploration techniques.
- Practice effective focus and control methods for inner exploration.
- Learn innovative spiritual development and exploration methods.
- Experience extensive guided Hemi-Sync® technology.
- Methods to have a profound spiritual experience.
- Experience an empowering fire ceremony.
- Unique and powerful healing methods.
- Learn how to effectively navigate thought-responsive environments.
- Practice powerful methods to reshape your reality.
- Unique and powerful healing methods.
- Learn methods to discover the answers for yourself.

THE DESTINATION: HIGHER SELF WORKSHOP

In many cultures and religions the process of death and dying is considered a powerful opportunity for spiritual liberation. What can you do today to enhance your spiritual journey of consciousness? In this program you will develop your own Spiritual Directive, learn the practices of an end-of-life coach, and experience techniques that will clear the way for you to achieve escape velocity from the dimensions of density and form.

For many the time has arrived to become spiritually self-empowered and break free from the limits of all belief systems. Learn how to take effective action and self-direct your awareness beyond the consensus realities of the astral dimension.

- Become knowledgeable about our continuing evolution beyond matter
- Assist loved ones in their journey of consciousness by identifying and removing emotional energy blocks
- Observe and apply the skills of an end-of-life doula
- Learn how to prepare for your ideal enlightened transition by recognizing and releasing attachments
- Practice techniques to control and direct your state of consciousness during altered states
- Create a sacred space to intensify the transition experience
- Learn about various nonphysical realities and how they function
- Address grief issues from a spiritual perspective
- Learn how to effectively navigate thought-responsive environments
- Experience extensive guided Hemi-Sync® exercises

This workshop will enable you to design your final transition from physical reality. Prepare to make the most of your end-of-life spiritual journey. Death is just the beginning.

Instruction for this program is provided by William and Susan Buhlman. Bill is the best-selling author of <u>Adventures beyond the Body</u> and <u>Adventures in the Afterlife</u>. Susan is a hospice volunteer, a certified end-of-life doula and bereavement coach. For more information visit, www.astralinfo.org.

Destination: Higher Self CD Set

AFFIRMATIONS FOR AN ENLIGHTENED TRANSITION

One powerful method of enhancing the transition of consciousness is to incorporate spiritual affirmations as a mantra and focus on your highest spiritual intention. Repeat and maintain your intention as your last conscious thought. Play this recording at the bedside during your own or a loved one's pending transition. Program your audio device for repeat play at a soft volume.

The goal is to focus your entire state of consciousness upon your spiritual essence beyond all form-based realities. Repetition of the phrases is intentional. Spiritual self-empowerment through our personal intention is an effective way to accelerate the evolution of our consciousness. The terms God, source, or universe may be interchanged, depending upon your personal preference. Higher Self Now!

There are two CDs in this set. The first is _Affirmations to Experience your Higher Self._

Affirmations to Experience your Higher Self– This is a repetition of positive statements that encourage the subconscious to move beyond the physical body, into the spiritual essence of who we really are. This can be enjoyed during sleep, meditation or even an activity that allows for you to absorb the statements. Become one with the affirmations and hold your intention as your last conscious thought.

On CD 2 there are two meditations. One is called _Doorways to Your Higher Self,_ the other is _Waves of Light._

Doorways to Your Higher Self – The purpose of this meditation is to identify and remove the specific blocks that may be holding you back from achieving your higher self-awareness. It could be fear, guilt or attachment to a physical concept. This technique will assist you to not only address, but release the limit. Once through the doors you will systematically shed those attachments that keep you from attaining the spiritual experience that you desire.

Waves of Light – With each wave of light, you will feel yourself becoming less and less attached as you become one with the light. This will assist you in achieving your destination: your higher self.

Both CDs are supported with Hemi-Sync® technology. With each of these, you should be in a quiet place where you can focus on the technique. Keep a journal nearby so that you can record any insights that you gain during your meditative time.

William Buhlman

The author's forty years of extensive personal out-of-body explorations give him a unique and thought provoking insight into the unseen nature of reality. His first book, <u>Adventures beyond the Body</u> chronicles his personal journey of self-discovery through out-of-body travel, and provides the reader with the preparation and techniques that can be used for their own adventure.

He has conducted an international out-of-body experience survey that includes over 16,000 participants from forty-two countries. The provocative results of this survey are presented in his book, <u>The Secret of the Soul</u>. This cutting edge book explores the unique opportunities for personal growth and profound spiritual awakenings that are reported during out-of-body experiences.

Over the past two decades William has developed an effective system to experience safe, self-initiated out-of-body adventures. He conducts an in-depth six-day workshop titled, Out-of-Body Exploration Intensive at the renowned Monroe Institute in Virginia. As a certified hypnotherapist, William incorporates various methods, including hypnosis, visualization and meditation techniques in his workshops to explore the profound nature of out-of-body experiences and the benefits of accelerated personal development. Through lectures, workshops and his books the author teaches the preparation and techniques for out-of-body and spiritual exploration.

The author brings a refreshing look to how we can use the exploration of consciousness to explore our spiritual identity and enhance our intellectual and physical lives. William is best known for his ability to teach people how to have profound spiritual adventures through the use of out-of-body experiences and altered states of consciousness. In addition, he has developed an extensive series of audio programs that are designed to expand awareness and assist in the exploration of consciousness. William has appeared on hundreds of YouTube and radio shows worldwide.

William's books are currently available in twelve languages. The author lives in the USA. For more information visit the author's web site, www.astralinfo.org.

Susan Buhlman

Susan Buhlman is a hospice volunteer and a certified end-of-life doula. It is her passion and her soul's purpose to provide comfort to those who are actively dying. As a companion to those in the final hours or days of life, she offers a calming, compassionate presence and, if the patient is open to it, Susan guides him or her through a transitional preparation process. Guided visualizations, positive affirmations, Hemi-Sync® and energy healing are a few of the tools that are used to ease the emotional pain and fear of the dying process. As a coach during bereavement workshops, she uses spiritual principles to lessen the burden of loss, leading the way toward a peaceful appreciation of the next conscious steps in our soul's journey. For more information visit www.astralinfo.org.

Acknowledgements

*"At times our own light goes out and is rekindled by
a spark from another person. Each of us has cause to
think with deep gratitude of those who have lighted the
flame within us."*

ALBERT SCHWEITZER

THIS BOOK WOULD not have been possible without all the support
and involvement of many people and organizations.

Those that were approaching the end of this physical life
were very generous in allowing us to be a part of their journey.
We truly appreciate the invitation to participate in the most significant part of this incarnation, their spiritual transition. By
sharing their stories, they become the teachers for all of us.

Words are insufficient to describe the impact that hospice
organizations have on the dying and their loved ones. The
medical teams, counselors and volunteers are the most caring folks in the service to others. If the time comes for you to
consider this alternative, please take advantage of all they have
to offer. It is with this support, the dying can truly focus on
their journey. Many of these organizations are not for profit.

Any assistance to one of these organizations, whether time or financial, is a gift to those who are in their last hours of this physical life.

Special thanks to Nancy McMoneagle and The Monroe Institute in Faber, Virginia for their continuing support. It is with great appreciation we thank them for being a world leader in the exploration of consciousness. I encourage you to investigate their various workshops and programs held around the world. Visit them at www.monroeinstitute.org. I would also like to thank Patty Avalon and Penny Holmes for their wonderful assistance during my workshops at the Institute for the past six years.

My website is a product of the creative and inspiring work by Webbloomer.com. Thanks to Eric Buhlman, CEO of this full service web marketing company. (And to Becky who has been so supportive of the long hours spent on this project.)

Many thanks to Claudia Carlton Lambright (cclediting@ gmail.com) for her encouragement, thoughtful comments, and skillful editing. She has been very involved in providing support for the OBE community for many years, and it is a privilege to have her as our editor on this project.

Thanks to the Monroe Products team for supporting and publishing the _Destination: Higher Self_ and the _Out-of-Body Exploration_ audio programs.

I would like to thank all the participants of my workshops, _Destination: Higher Self_ and _Out-of-body Exploration Intensive_ for making such them fun and memorable events. You have provided valuable shared experiences and encouragement. I am grateful for all of your input and validation. And of course the workshops were only possible with the help of the entire TMI support team.

My appreciation goes out to the Path 11 production team (Michael Habernig and April Hannah) for your hard work and dedication to the Path video series. Your team has a unique approach in providing information and encouragement to those who are seeking support for their own spiritual evolution.

Printed in Poland
by Amazon Fulfillment
Poland Sp. z o.o., Wrocław

31543767R00188